The Devil's Playground

The Devil's Playground

Inside America's Defense of the Deadly Korean DMZ

Gary L. Bloomfield

Guilford, Connecticut

An imprint of The Rowman & Littlefield Publishing Group, Inc.
4501 Forbes Blvd., Ste. 200
Lanham, MD 20706
www.rowman.com

Distributed by NATIONAL BOOK NETWORK

Copyright © 2019 Gary L. Bloomfield

British Library Cataloguing in Publication Information available

Library of Congress Cataloging-in-Publication Data available
Names: Bloomfield, Gary L., author.
Title: The devil's playground : inside America's defense of the deadly Korean DMZ / Gary Bloomfield.
Description: Guilford, Connecticut : Lyons Press, [2019] | Includes bibliographical references and index.
Identifiers: LCCN 2019007646 | ISBN 9781493039029 (cloth : alk. paper) | ISBN 9781493039036 (electronic)
Subjects: LCSH: Korean Demilitarized Zone (Korea)—History. | Military assistance, American—Korea (South) | United States—Armed Forces—Korea (South)—History. | Korea (South)—Defenses. | Korea (North)—Defenses.
Classification: LCC DS921.7 .B56 2019 | DDC 355/.0330519—dc23 LC record available at https://lccn.loc.gov/2019007646

♾™ The paper used in this publication meets the minimum requirements of American National Standard for Information Sciences—Permanence of Paper for Printed Library Materials, ANSI/NISO Z39.48-1992.

To the thousands of American and South Korean soldiers who have served along the DMZ, and the hundreds who have died, brutally, in provocative incidents *after* the Armistice Agreement was signed in 1953.

To Kim Yong-kyn, my roommate and translator when he was a KATUSA soldier, who accompanied me on so many trips to the DMZ and other perilous stops (such as a leper colony)—who took the time to show me his beautiful country and its people, and whom I will never forget.

To Sheppard Kelly, my NCOIC in the 2nd Infantry Division public affairs office, who expected me to do my best, all the time, and who taught me that every single person is unique and has a story to tell. More than anyone else, he has influenced me as an Army photojournalist and after I retired, as a military author.

And to Galen Geer, "The Lump." Vietnam veteran and outdoorsman, who felt more comfortable stomping around the DMZ than back in the office. Who said I'd never amount to much as a writer until I learned to drink scotch, smoke a pipe, and wear a tweed jacket with patches on the elbows. Got the jacket, but I've never smoked or drank. Maybe that's why it took nearly twenty more years before my first book. Galen was my inspiration to think big picture and run the gauntlet of writing books.

Contents

Author's Notes

$\mathcal{A}$fter twenty-seven months living in South Korea, many more years fondly recalling the many friends I made and who I will never forget, the powder keg situation there is of constant concern. In writing this book I use the terms that have several variations. For continuity I have changed them to the following words and phrases:

Korean names. The family name always proceeds one or two first names. For example, South Korea's former President Park (family name), Chung Hee (first name). He would be called President Park, not President Hee.

ROK. The Republic of (South) Korea.

DPRK. The Democratic People's Republic of (North) Korea. To avoid confusion between ROK and DPRK I have, in most cases, used the terms South Korea and North Korea. Some sources write these two countries as north Korea and south Korea.

KATUSA. Korean Augmentee to the U.S. Army. Every eligible male in South Korea has to serve in the military. A select few serve alongside American servicemen and women, living in the same barracks, and eating in the same mess halls.

JOE CHINK. An obviously derogatory term used by GIs in Korea referring to North Korean infiltrators who torment them along the DMZ. It does not refer to Koreans, or Asians in general.

UNC. The United Nations Command. In South Korea, the UNC is composed almost entirely of U.S. officers and soldiers, which the North Koreans try to exploit to the fullest for propaganda purposes. The enlisted men, many who serve as security guards in the Joint Security Area at PanMunJom, are all volunteers. Military units from other countries rotate to South Korea for temporary duty, augmenting the UN force there.

PanMunJom. Another word that's used a variety of ways. Again for the sake of consistency I have changed all excerpts to this one style.

The Manchus. All U.S. Army battalions have a nickname. The soldiers of the 2nd Battalion, 9th Infantry are called the Manchus, a name chosen to remember the 2/9th's role in the Chinese Boxer Rebellion. They were stationed along the DMZ when I was there, though many other combat units have also served there.

The Demilitarized Zone (DMZ) and Military Demarcation Line (MDL). The DMZ is a gash that separates North from South Korea. It has minefields, barbed wire, guard posts, sentry posts, motion detectors, and so on. Allied forces control and patrol the southern sector of the zone; North Korea oversees the northern sector. The MDL is the actual line that separates north from south. It is little more than simple marker posts and it is very easy for patrols from either side to stray across the line, whether inadvertently or intentionally.

The Armistice Agreement ended the conflicts in the Korean War but was only a cease-fire. Technically the war has never ended.

The **Joint Security Area (JSA)** at PanMunJom is where delegates from both sides—the United Nations and North Korea—discuss issues about the Armistice, file violations about border incidents, plus issue countercharges and denials. Prior to August of 1976, military personnel from both sides were free to roam throughout the JSA, but a tragic event—the Tree Incident—changed the terms of the Armistice, and military personnel now remain on their respective side of the MDL.

Foreword

Michael F. Davino, Colonel, USA, Retired

$\mathcal{T}$oday, the Korean Peninsula remains a dangerous place, with the potential for a very violent and bloody conflict, a war that could kill millions of people.

As most readers know, the Korean War was undeclared. Today we read and hear much about presidents and their executive orders. This is nothing new. For the United States, the Korean War started with an order from President Harry Truman to commit forces to counter the unprovoked attack by North Korean forces on South Korea. After more than three years of bitter combat, an Armistice between military commanders took effect on July 27, 1953. But no peace treaty was ever signed.

Although the two Koreas remain technically at war, when President Dwight D. Eisenhower signed executive order number 10585, the Korean War ended for the United States, effective on January 31, 1955. Those service members who arrived in Korea after that date are not Korean War veterans. However, as is often heard in the U.S. military, "the enemy gets a vote." While the peninsula has been at relative peace since Ike signed his executive order, there have been streams of North Korean provocations. Ninety-two U.S. service members and forty-three Korean Augmentees to the U.S. Army have been killed during hostilities with North Korean forces since the Armistice, most of them during the late 1960s, when our country's armed forces were heavily committed in Vietnam. (Many more Republic of Korea and North Korean troops have been killed.)

Some of these attacks are fairly well known, like the seizure of the USS *Pueblo* and the infamous "axe murder" incident in PanMunJom. But many of the deaths are not, especially those men killed in hundreds of small-unit actions and firefights along the Korean Demilitarized Zone (DMZ) in the late 1960s, at a time when the war in Southeast Asia was at its peak.

Although the number of U.S. combat deaths in Korea after the Armistice is relatively small in relation to the total casualties of other conflicts, the impact on the family of each service member is the same, if not worse. When I served as president of the 2nd Indianhead Division Association, families and friends of the fallen contacted me, reaching out for information about 2nd Infantry Division veterans who served with their loved one. One family member wrote that she remembers that her family was somewhat relieved to hear that her brother was to be assigned to Korea, where the war was over, instead of Vietnam, where it was raging. That made it all the more shocking when the Army informed them that her brother was killed in a firefight with the North Koreans in 1968.

Another case, which shows how generally unaware the American public was of the continuing hostilities in Korea, was when I made a Freedom of Information Act request to help a friend of another 2nd Division soldier killed in action near the DMZ in 1967. I wanted his individual deceased personnel file. As I reviewed the file, I saw a request from the soldier's family that his headstone be marked "Korea." The funeral home director responded in a letter that there must be some kind of mistake. The soldier was born in 1948, so he could not have been killed in Korea. Sadly, the funeral director was badly misinformed.

Other service members from the late 1960s and early 1970s still suffer today from the effects of Agent Orange and other tactical herbicides that were spread near the Demilitarized Zone in an effort to clear the dense vegetation that North Korean agents were using to conceal their movements. Military service along the DMZ is inherently dangerous even in the absence of combat. Since July 27, 1954, more than 1,100 U.S. soldiers, sailors, airmen, and marines have been killed in training accidents, died of illnesses like the deadly Korean hemorrhagic fever, been lost in aircraft crashes, or died through many other causes on and near the Korean Peninsula.

During the sixty-five years since the Armistice, a U.S. Army general has been responsible for maintaining the Armistice agreement, and if deterrence fails, he is charged to lead the combined U.S. and Republic of Korea forces in combat, along with members of the nations that remain part of the UN Command. Since 1954, more than two million Americans have served on the Korean Peninsula, ready to "fight tonight," if necessary.

The importance of this residual force in Korea over the years cannot be understated. One need only look at the situation in Iraq, where the United States did not maintain a powerful presence, to understand. Our long-term commitment in Korea has allowed the Republic of Korea to transition from a dictatorship to a democratically elected government and grow into an economic powerhouse.

The last U.S. death at the hands of the North Koreans occurred in 1994, a few years after the United States withdrew the last of its infantry battalions from the DMZ. But since then, North Korea has developed into a nuclear weapons power, capable of threatening our allies in the region and perhaps even our own homeland. From time to time, it has engaged in armed clashes with South Korean forces, killing dozens of soldiers and sailors. So it is indeed fitting that Gary L. Bloomfield has carefully researched and documented the armed conflict that has gone for decades on the Korean Peninsula. It will help honor those veterans who have served in Korea since the Armistice and those who did not survive their assignment in that dangerous part of the world.

Sanford, North Carolina
Memorial Day, May 28, 2018

Introduction

Why I Wrote This Book

𝒯he flight from Tokyo to Kimpo Airport near Seoul, South Korea, is two hours, give or take a few, depending on whether the jet stream is turbulent or if it's monsoon season. Those who haven't experienced one, think of the monsoons as a heavy rainstorm. It's more like getting drenched with a barrel of water continuously for days on end. My flight was delayed and I got to Kimpo after hours and knew the Turtle Farm would be closed, so instead I caught a cab and checked into the Chosun Hotel for the night.

Downtown Seoul hadn't changed much in four years and I thought about hitting the streets though it was approaching eleven and curfew in an hour would bring most everything to a halt. Except the nightclubs and discos that lock their doors but stay open till morning since no one is allowed on the streets until dawn. With a captive audience, the clubs jack up the prices on drinks and snacks. (Supposedly the curfew, at least back then in the 1970s, was so ROK Army units could reposition without spying eyes noticing the move.) I still had jet lag from the day before, flying from Kansas City to Tokyo, and really needed to get some sleep, because the next morning I had to check in at the Replacement Depot—the Turtle Farm—to find out where my next assignment would be.

I hoped I'd be in Seoul, maybe as editor for the Yongsan garrison newspaper again, or maybe as a journalist for the U.S. Forces Korea *KORUS*. I thought it might be too much to ask to latch onto the *Stars and Stripes* bureau. To me, it didn't much matter which job I got, as long as I could stay in Seoul. I had numerous friends from before, and they already knew I was coming back.

I reported to the personnel clerk promptly at 0800 the next morning, and he checked the roster for my name.

"Bloomfield, Gary L., Specialist 5, 71Q40-J8. What the hell MOS is that?"

"The 71Q40 is for newspaper editor, and the J-8 is photojournalist."

"Cool, Man. Says here you're going to the 2nd Infantry Division, PAO."

"Are you sure? I thought I'd be somewhere here in Seoul."

"Most of the other newbies here are eleven bang bangs, all going to 2nd ID, but yeah, you got tagged, only REMF on the inbound roster. There's a notation from the NCOIC, a SFC Sheppard Kelly, says if you don't take it, you can stay here . . . as a clerk typist, but that he'll ensure you never work as a journalist or editor again. Not sure I'd wanna be working for someone like that."

I actually contemplated the career change for about a minute, just so I could stay in Seoul, but reluctantly agreed to the offer, not that it was much of a choice. It took a few hours to arrange for my monthly pay allotment sent home, increase my life insurance, fill out a will, and check my shots. The whole time I'm wondering who in hell was this guy Kelly? I'd heard or seen his name before, one of those hot shots in D.C., annual award-winner for journalism excellence.

A quick lunch at the chow hall, then all of us caught the military bus north to Camp Casey, headquarters for the Indianhead Division. It took about two hours to get there and to pass through two checkpoints, with armed Korean soldiers walking down the aisle, spot-checking everyone. I was used to it, having been there a few years before, but some of the new guys didn't know what to think, and made snippy comments to the soldier checking IDs. I knew better than to mess with these guys, who don't have any sense of humor, and take their jobs very seriously, primarily looking for North Korean infiltrators. Initially everyone on the bus was shooting the shit, but as we got farther north and passed the telltale signs of a war zone, it got real quiet.

Just inside the gate at Camp Casey was an M60 tank with its crew standing off in the shade. Locked and loaded if the sirens went off. We were dropped off at the Adjutant General's office for more in-processing.

While waiting for my pay, sitting there with a dozen other soldiers, some of them nodding off from the jet lag and the boredom, the front door banged open and a wiry SFC walked in and bellowed, "BLOOMFIELD! Get yer ass over here!"

I didn't have to guess that this was probably Kelly. I wondered if it was too late to take that clerk typist job back in Seoul.

"Grab your bags. Let's go!"

"I'm waiting for my pay."

Kelly looked around the room, spotted the pay window and ripped into the pay clerk.

"Get Bloomfield paid NOW. We got to go."

A few minutes later we were in the PAO jeep, roaring down the main road on Camp Casey. Not one word was said during the five-minute drive. We pulled up to a lime-green Quonset hut. Outside was a sign: "2nd Inf. Div PAO, and Indianhead Newspaper, Second to None." Next door was the division museum.

"This is your home for the next thirteen months. Grab your duffel and I'll show you where your bunk is."

"I have to sign in with the company first."

"Nope. It's better if they don't know you're here. As soon as they know, you'll be doing morning PT, every day at 0530, once a week with full pack, helmet, and weapon. And once a month you'll pull CQ [charge of quarters, which is like a night watch in the barracks]. You got too many things to do to be worrying about that company nonsense."

I trusted that he knew what he was talking about, though I wondered how long I could remain off the books.

Quick introductions as everyone was leaving for the day, and a walk-through, side-shuffling through the photo lab, and back to the dungeon where our bunks were. I had to crawl over a bunk to get to mine tucked in the back corner. There were some boxes of typing paper and other supplies stacked on the mattress, which I stacked in the corner. I started to unpack my duffel but Kelly shouted from the outer office that I could do that when it was time to sack out. Late in the afternoon I was getting hungry, but I didn't have a meal card (since I hadn't checked in with the company) so I wasn't sure what Kelly had planned to eat.

"We've got a camp stove if you want C-rats or ramen, or we can go to the Korean Café half mile from here, which has great food, cheap." Hadn't had C-rations since deploying to Germany for war games the year before, while I was stationed at Fort Riley.

"What about the mess hall? I don't have a meal card but can't we pay for it?"

"You don't want to show your face there. Someone will be asking who you are."

It had been a long day and I was ready to crash, but I needed a shower. After a bowl of ramen, and a quick walk around the Q-hut so I'd know where everything was, I peeked in the latrine but all I saw was a sink and the stool. Kelly was at his desk reading teletype news flashes. "Whatchoo want now?"

"I'd like to be able to take a shower but didn't notice one here in the building." I was afraid he'd tell me to find the hose out back.

"I go to the . . ." and he pointed out the window, but then he got up and led me to the front door and pointed to another Quonset hut about a hundred yards away. It was down a rocky hill, across a ditch, and up another hill.

"Do not go up to the barracks because, just like at the mess hall, if someone sees you, they'll wanna know who you are."

I really didn't feel like making that trek to the shower, especially knowing I'd probably get dirty on the walk back. And, that's exactly what happened. I immediately decided that maybe a shower once a week would suffice.

Before sacking out for the night, Kelly informed me that tomorrow was a duty day, and he liked to get to work around seven, before the phones started ringing and anyone else could stop by to pester him. Plus, he didn't trust our house boy and wanted to keep an eye on him as he cleaned the building.

"I should sign in at the company, and get my weapon and my gear."

"Stop worrying about that stuff. I'll take care of it when I have time."

Before sacking out, that first night back in Korea, I dug through my duffel bag and pulled out my journal. Over the years I've learned to jot down my thoughts during the moment, not days or even hours later:

JOURNAL

For the next year I have no control over my life. No influence, nor say-so, for I am an American soldier stationed with the 2nd Infantry Division near the Devil's Playground, the Demilitarized Zone, in South Korea.

Everything here, and every day in, day out focuses on combat, our unit readiness for war, and the potential of an ever-impending invasion by North Korean troops only a few miles away. The only thing that separates us is a few coils of concertina wire and minefields.

It's a sobering feeling that is shared by many American soldiers who've never been in combat. Some were too young to know or even care about Vietnam, so the closest they've been to combat is basic training—hardly a notable "prep school" for the tough-guy tactics they may someday encounter with North Korean soldiers intent on killing them. Fresh out of high school, thrown directly into the line of fire, many rosy-cheeked and wide-eyed teenage GIs stationed on the Z will mature to twice their age by the time they leave, if they survive long enough to leave the zone. During my last tour, I was stationed at Yongsan, in Seoul, and I often saw Indianhead soldiers who looked battle-hardened from being on the Z too long. That was 1972. Now I'm back in Korea, this time with the 2nd Division. And here it's a completely different world. We are not at war, but it's still a combat zone. It's an uneasy peace in Korea, and many American soldiers, just as I, only hope their tour passes safely, without incident.

I quickly learned that if Kelly got to work at seven, he expected me to do likewise, as long as I didn't pester him. So instead I sat at my desk that first morning, checked whatever supplies and files were in the drawers, read a couple of stories slated for the next issue of the division newspaper and watched Mr. Kim clean the office.

I said "*On young, haw shim nee kaw?*" (Hello and how are you?) and it surprised him that I knew Korean. Many GIs don't bother, but it was my second tour and after spending nearly every day at an orphanage in Seoul, I had to learn a little just to communicate with the children.

Mr. Kim looked to be in his forties, maybe fifties, slightly hunched over, leather skin from too much sun. He wore khaki shorts, a torn Army t-shirt and flip flops. He started with the venetian blinds and the window sills, dusting them with a wet wash towel, then he emptied the trash cans, and flattened all the soda cans, and put all the newspapers and balled up typing paper in neat piles. I guessed he was making a little extra from recycling them.

Mr. Kim wiped out the ash trays with that towel, rinsed it out often to wipe off all the desks and file cabinets, then he went into the latrine and scrubbed the sink and the toilet. The last thing he did was empty and scrub the coffee pot, and an assortment of coffee mugs, and yes, with that same nasty towel.

I don't drink coffee or tea, fortunately. I never have. When I mentioned Mr. Kim's cleaning habits to another journalist, he just shrugged and said it probably added a little flavor to the coffee. I went back to the dungeon and dug out my shot record, to ensure my tetanus was up to date, just in case.

By eight everyone stumbled in, including the small group of Korean Army soldiers who would work on the Korean language pages of our newspaper. These soldiers who work with us are called KATUSAs—Korean Augmentees to the U.S. Army, and they would quickly become my most trusted friends.

We were just chatting, me trying to impress them with my broken Korean, when SFC Kelly interrupted us, and pointed at me. "Let's go. Got someone you need to meet."

Kelly is long and lanky and always in a rush to get somewhere fast, so like a dutiful puppy, I had to trot to keep up with him as we trekked up the road, and walked into the headquarters building for the 2nd Infantry Division. I didn't have a clue where he was taking me, and by the time I figured it out, it was too late. He knocked at an open door and peeked in.

"Hey Kelly. C'mon in."

"Sir, I'd like to introduce you to Specialist Bloomfield, our new editor."

Sitting at the desk was Major General Morris Brady, commander of the 2nd Infantry Division. To say I was a little tongue-tied was an understatement.

"Good morning . . . Sir. Happy to meet you."

"Bloomfield. Bloomfield? I just read something about you." I figured maybe he'd seen some of the things I'd written for the Fort Riley *POST* newspaper, or maybe for *Soldiers* magazine. The CG shuffled some papers on his desk then found what he was looking for.

"Here it is. Morning report. Says you're AWOL."

"No, sir," Kelly chimed in. He gave me a look that implied I not say a word. "I picked him up late in the afternoon and by the time we got to the company, the orderly room was closed. Planning to get him signed in as soon as we're done here."

Somehow he believed him. "Just take care of it, Kelly."

"Yes, sir."

"Bloomfield . . . Army PAO says the *Indianhead* is a Class C newspaper, the only one in the whole Army. That's B.S. Everything I do is first class, and so I brought Kelly here to get it straightened out and he asked for you by name to get the paper up to an A rating. Understand?"

"Yes, sir. I'll do my best," I blurted out without a clue how to accomplish that on my own. I also figured it might not be a good time to mention I really wanted to be in Seoul. Actually, I never considered asking once I knew what the CG and Kelly expected of me.

"Kelly and I got about six months left in country, so that's how long you've got to turn this thing around. Sooner the better."

"Yes, sir."

"And I better not see your name on the morning report tomorrow, otherwise you'll be writing the newspaper from the stockade. Now get outta here."

"Yes, sir." I saluted him and backed out. Kelly hung back and I saw the two of them smiling at each other, like maybe I'd just been played. Little did I know that over the next six months they both tormented the hell out of me, sometimes playing good cop, bad cop, sometimes double-teaming me, often pissing me off to the max. Of course it was many years later that Sheppard Kelly finally confessed that they were working together to make me a better journalist and newspaper editor:

When Specialist Fifth Class Gary Bloomfield arrived in South Korea to become the editor of the 2nd Infantry Division's newspaper, the supervisory staff in the office in which he was to work already knew him to be an accomplished, prolific writer, from reading his articles in his stateside Army newspaper. We were unaware, however, that he had spent a previous tour in Seoul—some 40 miles south of his new duty station. The newspaper he was to edit had the previous year been given a "C" grade by the Department of the Army—the lowest grade given. It was given to newspapers that served their readership little of the time. Some of the judging criteria were how well the newspapers entertained, informed and educated the soldiers. The *Indianhead* was said to fall short in the latter two areas.

The division commander had mandated that the paper be brought up to class A quickly, saying, "If you aren't going first class, there is no point in going at all." Initially Gary seemed more interested in writing than editing. He had arrived with some preconceived notions, based on his prior experiences, about relations between Koreans and American soldiers. He seemed intent on bettering those relations, and spent a considerable amount of his free time interviewing the civilians in the nearby village of Tong Du Chon. A do-it-yourself kind of person, Gary would take on the tougher interviews himself. As a military editor, however, it was his responsibility to teach and supervise the journalists assigned to staff. This included five or six U.S. military journalists and three to five KATUSAs—Korean soldiers who augmented the staff. They also wrote two pages of the newspaper in the Korean language for the KATUSAs who augmented organizations throughout the division.

It took quite a bit of arm twisting to get Gary to spend more time in his editor's chair. At that point, he was still developing as an editor, supervisor and teacher. Instead of correcting writers' errors himself, he taught them to correct their own. The newspaper also started telling why and how division soldiers did what they did. That required book and newspaper research, something the staff seemed to despise. The resultant stories were a vast improvement over those previously presented, and within three or four months the paper was given an "A" rating. Then came a special newspaper about the KATUSAs, how the program came into being and their melding into the division's fighting plan. This required that Gary and the writers learn as much as possible about the Korean War, and post Korean War period. It was probably the best single issue of any newspaper published in Korea that year.

The improvement was borne out during the judging of all the military newspapers a few months later in which the *Indianhead* won about three-quarters of the awards available. Gary's growth didn't stop there. The greatest change I saw was in his attitude following his first trip up to the Demilitarized Zone, a stone's throw away from our compound. It was a trip he really did not want to make. Galen Geer, a Vietnam War vet, assigned to the office, accompanied him. Upon his return to the division, whose soldiers guard the Demilitarized Zone, it seemed that he had a greater appreciation for the relationship between the division soldiers and civilians in the local village. While most of the men in the village provided daily logistical support of various types to the division, they shared the same dangers as the division soldiers should an attack from the north take place.

Over these many years Gary's books show a love for research, something that was either non-existent or well hidden upon his arrival at the division, in 1977.

Looking back I didn't always appreciate SFC Kelly overseeing the improvements to the newspaper or his molding of the staff, which often had other priorities that took place after hours. More than too often SFC Kelly berated all of us to get out there and do our jobs. But during those six months of hell, we turned the *Indianhead* around, and finally got that A rating the CG demanded. And along the way we garnered a bunch of awards, including U.S. Forces Korea "Best Newspaper." Several of our stories were singled out, and I was selected Army Journalist of the Year and United Nations Command Best Journalist. Though Major General Brady had already moved on to another assignment by then, when he heard the news about my awards, he sent me a telegram, saying he was "busting proud." I couldn't help but look back on all we'd done to transform the *Indianhead* into an award-winning newspaper and recalled the popular quote, "The difficult we do every day. The impossible takes a little longer."

At about this same time, a peanut farmer from Georgia decided to run for president and one of his campaign promises was to pull all U.S. troops out of Korea. It was a bone-headed idea, but no one took him seriously, until he became president. I had too many friends in Korea—the children at the orphanage in Seoul who called me Gary opa (older brother), the college students I taught conversational English to, and of course the KATUSAs I worked with and roomed with and who showed me their beautiful country. I knew I had to do something and decided to write a book about Korea and the DMZ and the soldiers who are stationed there.

It took two years to complete the book and, because I was still in the Army, I had to submit the manuscript for *Devil's Playground* to the Pentagon for approval. Took about six months and when I got it back, it was shredded, with only about half of it approved. The rest was stamped "classified," even though I was careful to use only nongovernment sources such as national newspapers and magazines, and book excerpts. I knew there was no sense arguing about it. My next assignment in Germany was as part of the U.S. Army Europe News Team, and I didn't have time to massage *Devil's Playground*, so I shelved it, leaving it at my parent's house in Kansas City.

Twenty years later I'd left the Army, gotten my bachelor's and master's degrees on the GI Bill, been managing editor for *VFW* magazine, edited two books on World War II, and written two books—on World War II athletes and entertainers. My publisher asked if I had anything else in the works. I mentioned a book I'd done on Korea and the DMZ and he asked to see it, so I dusted it off, salvaged what was left of it after the Pentagon hatchet job, and reworked it. He liked it but said there was no interest at that time in Korea, so I set it aside again. Late in 2017, after I just finished two books—on George Patton and Mark Twain—my publisher asked if I still had that Korea book and that now might be a great time to release it.

Once again I dusted off *Devil's Playground*, decided to scrap practically everything except the title, a few of the chapters and my journal notes and photos. Then I wrote a totally new book. I'd been filing away newspaper and magazine articles, book excerpts and declassified documents about Korea and the DMZ, just in case there was ever any interest in Korea, so I had plenty of new material. I didn't want this book to be just another think-tank piece, but rather more about the troops on the ground, those stationed on the DMZ, and how decisions (and indecisions) in D.C., Pyongyang and Seoul, and Tokyo, Beijing and Moscow impact them, because, if war does break out on the Korean Peninsula, if North Korea finally attempts to achieve its goal of reunifying Korea as a communist state, it's those American servicemen and women stationed north of Seoul, who will be, who know they will be the trip wire that ensures American involvement in the war that ended with a cease-fire.

When the Armistice Agreement was signed in 1953, ending the Korean Conflict, our boys came home, my father included, peace was restored and Korea became the forgotten war. While America turned its attention to other hot spots, to Berlin and Cuba, and Southeast Asia, North Korea was preparing to finish a war that never ended, and they vowed to reunify the peninsula, no matter what it cost, no matter what sacrifices had to be made. Not much has been heard from the region these past many decades, certainly nothing to become overly concerned about. Sure there have been minor incidents that get mentioned on the inside pages, but very few make it to the banner headlines.

There was the seizure of the intelligence ship *Pueblo*, the Tree Incident at PanMunJom, several assassination attempts on the South Korean presidents and the shoot-downs of a Korean Airlines passenger plane and an American spy plane, but beyond these few incidents, the American public heard little about Korea. That is until recently when two inexperienced leaders—a newly elected American president, and an untested grandson of North Korea's Great Leader squared off in the world arena, both threatening to unleash a firestorm of missiles and destroy each other.

Koreans on both sides of the Demilitarized Zone have never felt lasting peace was restored on the peninsula. It is a powder keg. Always has been, we were just concerned with other issues and other parts of the world, until now.

While the United States has sent troops to Bosnia and Somalia, Panama, Grenada and Mogadishu, Iraq and Afghanistan, North Korea has been taking shots at our service members stationed there all along, and even though they want us gone, they won't push us off the peninsula.

I was one of those young soldiers sent over to Korea, for two eye-opening tours in the 1970s that had such an impact on me, I wrote a series of articles about a country and a situation that has always been smoldering—occasionally verging on exploding into an inferno, pushing us perilously close to World War III.

I'm not a politician, a diplomat, or a high-ranking officer who studied military history and understands battle strategies. I'm just a former soldier who still has friends in Korea I care deeply about. Maybe I have a little more insight because of my curiosity as a military journalist who has been there, on the DMZ, and seen the threat up close.

For those of us who have been there, we know it hasn't changed during all this time. Certainly, Seoul has become an amazingly vibrant city of millions, one of the crown jewels of Asia, while Pyongyang may appear to outsiders as a metropolis but it's really nothing more than a Potemkin Village. But for all of its accomplishments as a world leader, Seoul is still within artillery range of the border, and would suffer enormous losses in the opening days if hostilities resume. That threat has always been very real, but North Korea's development of nukes escalates that concern. There is little doubt the combined forces of South Korea and the United States would eventually win any war with North Korea, but the devastation to Seoul would be enormous and the loss of life could be in the millions, and for that reason alone, war must be avoided at all costs.

I can relate only what I saw and experienced during my two tours. Yet even today, every time another incident flares, every time North Korea makes the news, I know the situation is actually much worse than what is being reported. And if anyone foolishly believes that somehow the situation over there has subsided, recently North Korea issued this damning statement in early 2017: "The army and people . . . with burning hatred for the Yankees are in full readiness to fight a death-defying battle."

"Burning hatred for the Yankees" doesn't sound much like a peace overture to me, but it also doesn't sound any different from the rhetoric I heard in the seventies or have read all these many years since.

Seeing the hatred in their eyes, it's easy for me to understand that even the lowliest of North Korean soldier would be instantly elevated to hero status if they killed an American soldier. Serving along Korea's Demilitarized Zone is not to be taken lightly.

In the 1960s and early '70s, war in Vietnam overshadowed anything happening in Korea. In recent years, war in Iraq and Afghanistan is certainly more dangerous for our men and women in uniform, but serving in Korea is hardly a cushy job.

While the politicians and diplomats in Washington, D.C., and at the United Nations in New York, in the capitols of Seoul, Pyongyang, Beijing, Tokyo, and Moscow issue statements warning of a nuclear holocaust in northeast Asia, our American soldiers stationed in Korea are the ones I think of most—for they would suffer the immediate consequences, along with the millions of innocent civilians in Seoul, if war breaks out. Among those innocent civilians are my former "sisters" from the orphanage I spent so much time at, the college students I debated with while helping them with their conversational English, and of course the KATUSA soldiers I worked with, and befriended. All of them never far from my mind, every day.

During a debate with college students in June 1978, while sitting around a tea room in Seoul, I was asked what I thought of North Korea. I explained it simply: "On the international stage, North Korea blusters with a superiority attitude, to hide an inferiority complex."

I still feel that way, only now they've got nukes, as if that somehow gives them legitimacy on the world stage. They think it does, but the bulk of their military—those thousands of tanks and artillery pieces, the hundreds of fighter planes—are vintage 1960s or even older. But even with modern fighter jets, tanks and submarines from Russia and China, they lack spare parts and fuel, which would limit their offensive capabilities to weeks, possibly only days before our military superiority would seize the initiative and obliterate anything and everything they've got.

When the 2nd Infantry Division manned the DMZ, Guard Post Ouellette was only a few yards from the Military Demarcation Line, making it an easy target for enemy infiltrators to throw rocks and sometimes hand grenades at the lookout posts, and do it without crossing into South Korea. Photo by Gary L. Bloomfield.

The first time I went to the DMZ, I was a little bit apprehensive and it obviously showed. Photo by Galen Geer.

In the Demilitarized Zone separating North from South Korea, it is deadly serious business, this game of stare-down along the Military Demarcation Line. Every once in a while it escalates to fisticuffs and firefights and skirmishes and even though the 2nd Infantry Division has since been pulled back further south, relinquishing DMZ duties to the ROKs, there are still American military police troops assigned to the Joint Security Area at PanMunJom, and U.S. military personnel representing the UN Command at the Truce Village, where confrontations can flare at any time, without warning.

For those of us who have been there, this beautiful country is known as something more sinister than The Land of the Morning Calm. The Demilitarized Zone, that barren gash, lined with barbed-wire fencing and minefields, guard towers and foot patrols, the most heavily armed confrontation in the world, is known as The Devil's Playground.

Overview

Still Standing Guard in Korea

It is a riddle, wrapped in a mystery, inside an enigma. —Winston
Churchill on October 1, 1939, referring to Russia, but he could
just as easily have been referring to North Korea over the past
half century.

Author's Note: When I was managing editor for *VFW* magazine, I wrote the
following for the June/July 1990 issue.

"*H*umpin' the Yamas" is what American soldiers stationed in South Korea
call patrolling within the Demilitarized Zone (DMZ). Though the frequency
of North Korean provocations has subsided inside the Z, every patrol is warned
to remain rock steady because a firefight could erupt at any time, without
warning. All of their senses are trying to detect any sign of Communist infiltration. They listen, despite the distant North Korean artillery reverberations
(which mask underground explosions needed to construct invasion tunnels).

Only yards away, on the other side of the Military Demarcation Line
(which is little more than a chain of posts) 151 miles long, concealed North
Korean guerrillas often whistle or throw rocks, hoping to unnerve the young
American soldiers, prodding them to fire across the MDL, which would be
a major violation of the truce accords that signaled the end of the fighting in
the Korean War.

This daily badgering becomes more a battle of wits than of war. But despite its misnomer, the Korean Demilitarized Zone has the most potent arsenals in the world concentrated on every South Korean, U.S. and Communist
unit within or adjacent to its three-mile-wide swath that severs Korea in two.

Radical students and political dissidents in South Korea believe the U.S.
presence along the DMZ is preventing the reunification of North and South.

Communist propagandists have been spouting that same message for years, accusing the American "warmongers" of dominating and controlling each "puppet regime" in Seoul.

While it's true that the fifth largest army in the world is based on the Korean Peninsula, that army is, in fact, North Korea's, not America's, which has only 45,000 U.S. troops there to complement the Republic of (South) Korea's 650,000 man defense forces. The allies' combined strength would have to repel more than a million Communist troops spearheaded by a 100,000-man commando force.

Though the U.S./ROK forces maintain a heightened readiness posture, it is to repel an attack, not instigate one. The North, on the other hand, has had one goal since the truce agreement in 1953—to eliminate the U.S. presence, reunify the country (by force if necessary), and impose Communism on the new Korea.

With a 2-to-1 advantage in tanks, artillery, and fighter jets, a 3-to-1 edge in naval warships, an entire populace, including women and children willing to die for their god-like hero/leader Kim Il Sung, North Korea certainly has the war machine to attempt an attack, though analysts doubt they could sustain it without substantial Soviet or Chinese support.

But China is abandoning the stagnant and deteriorating North in favor of economically powerful South Korea. As recently as 1989, China had established a $3 billion trade agreement with South Korea, but only a sixth as much ($500 million) with North Korea.

The Soviet Union and its European satellites are finally listening to the masses, who are hungry for change, adopting varying forms of democracy and capitalism, leaving Communist stalwarts like Kim Il Sung and Cuba's Fidel Castro on a precarious ledge without their accustomed security blanket. In years past the Communist super power leaders begrudgingly tolerated the fanaticism of Kim Il Sung, a hard-line Stalinist devotee who refuses to allow the dramatic changes that have occurred in East Europe and China to occur in his isolated bastion of Communism.

The rapid changes that have occurred in Europe have prompted a call for a reduction of U.S. forces worldwide. But while a reciprocal reduction will likely take place among the Soviets and other Warsaw Pact forces, no such move is promised by the North Koreans.

In fact, U.S. and South Korean military leaders and politicians emphasize that any wholesale reduction would be foolhardy, and might even encourage the dying North Korean dictator to rally his disciples for one last loyalty show, urging them to invade the South and fulfill his last wish! U.S. and South Korean leaders, ever-wary of the North Korean threat, are proposing numerous changes that will strengthen, not weaken, the allied forces.

- By 1992 South Korea will have completed a major military moderniza- tion program, which will include building its own advanced combat aircraft. The three U.S. air bases in South Korea would be phased down as the ROKs gear up.
- Currently the headquarters for the United Nations Command, U.S. Forces Korea and 8th Army is in downtown Seoul. A move further south, paid for by South Korea, would free-up this prime piece of real estate and give the military command group more of a buffer from any North Korean attack.
- Maintaining the 45,000 U.S. troops in South Korea costs $2.6 billion annually. Now that South Korea is enjoying prosperity, it has agreed to pick up a larger share of that tab.
- Since the cease-fire, an American four-star general has commanded the unified U.S./ROK defense forces, Eventually that, and numerous subordinate positions, will be held by South Korean commanders.
- As part of the total manpower reduction throughout the Department of Defense, an estimated 7,000 noncombat troops (none from the forward- based 2nd Infantry Division) can be withdrawn from South Korea over the next few years, creating a "leaner, meaner, fighting machine."

For the infantrymen of the 2nd Division, who love "humpin' the yamas" and who confront and deal with North Korean aggression every day, they know their role as a trip wire is vital to preserving the peace in Korea.

U.S. and South Korean politicians and military leaders fully intend to show the American Flag along the DMZ for years to come, and to keep that "caged animal" (North Korea) from straying outside its wasteland. The Soviet Union and China are further ostracizing Kim Il Sung, forcing him to either change with the times, or die of isolation.

Until the change occurs, the U.S. remains committed to the security of South Korea.

• *1* •

An Olympic Hero

Sport is war minus the shooting. —George Orwell, 1945

JOURNAL

I ran track in junior high school—hundred yard dash, quarter-mile, and half-mile. Tried to be a miler and even cross-country runner but hated it. Even ran both low and high hurdles and tossed the discus. Then in basic training, we ran two miles every morning, in combat boots, airborne shuffle all the way. I was a squad leader. Didn't dare fall out, even when my chest felt like it might explode, and I couldn't breathe in that heavy Fort Polk summer heat. In Korea, we ran during the monsoon rains, and winter snowstorms and I hated running even more, but I've always admired those who can gut it out, and barely break sweat.

$\mathcal{A}t$ the 1988 Summer Olympic Games in Seoul, marathon runner Sohn Kee Chung entered Jamil Stadium alone and circled the track for a long overdue victory lap. This native son, born in the Pyongan region of North Korea, raised his arms and waved to the crowd, all of them on their feet, cheering him on, chanting as he crossed the finish line.

It had been a very long journey for Sohn, and his story, filled with bitterness and shame, was a microcosm of Korea's history in the twentieth century.

Treaties in 1904 and 1907 made Korea a protectorate of Imperial Japan. By 1910, Japan was in full control of Korea and moved swiftly to abolish the Korean language, culture, and history. Sohn was born in 1912 (some records say it was 1914) and he was forced to speak Japanese and learn about Japanese history. National sites and cultural paintings and statues throughout the

17

country were defaced and destroyed, virtually obliterating all traces of Korea's illustrious history. Isolated protests were met with imprisonments and mass executions. Schoolchildren were taught Japanese history and culture and were required to speak only Japanese.

As a boy, Sohn would race his friends on foot as they rode their bikes, then later he trained in Seoul, where his track coach made him run with stones and sacks of sand strapped to his back. Sohn initially ran the 1,500 meter and 5,000 meter races, but by 1933 he chose the longer distances and won his first eight-miler that year, then set his sights on marathons, competing in twelve between 1933 and 1936, winning nine races and consistently finishing in the top three.

In November 1935, in Tokyo, Sohn had set the world marathon record of two hours and twenty-six minutes. He qualified for the upcoming Summer Olympics in Berlin, but he would have to run for Japan, not his Korean homeland, and because Japan required everyone in the occupied peninsula to use Japanese names, Sohn would run as Son Kitei. (Another Korean marathon runner—Nam Seung Yong—also qualified for the Japanese team.)

In Berlin, Sohn was leading the pack when he entered the Olympic Stadium, but when he looked up at the scoreboard, he saw instead the name Son Kitei, with the symbol of the Japanese flag next to it. Sohn won the gold medal, while Nam took the bronze. On the medal stand, they both bowed their heads as the Japanese flag was raised, and as they listened to the Japanese national anthem. Both Korean athletes were humiliated to be representing a country that had treated their fellow Koreans with disdain. Sohn told reporters that he stood on the medal stand feeling "shame and outrage." During press conferences, he tried explaining his Korean heritage to reporters, but his Japanese minders conveniently altered his words, saying he was proud to represent Japan.

Days later, the Korean newspaper *Dong-a Ilbo* ran a photo of Sohn and obliterated the Japanese flag on the front of his track vest. This blatant defacing of the Rising Sun incensed the Japanese occupiers, and eight members of the newspaper staff were imprisoned and the publication was suspended for nine months.

At the same time that Adolf Hitler was expanding his Thousand-Year Reich across Europe, Japan was stretching its tentacles into Manchuko and southeast Asia, tapping into oil reserves, rubber plantations, iron ore and magnesium deposits, all vital to sustaining their rapidly developing war machine. Of the two regions of Korea, Japan mined the north's wealth of natural mineral deposits, while the south was considered the breadbasket, with lush, fertile lowlands. Japan also established clandestine labs and facilities in the northern

Sohn Kee Chung ran marathons in the Far East and qualified for the 1936 Berlin Olympics. He won the gold medal but the win was bittersweet because, instead of representing Korea, he ran for Japan, which occupied his home country. More than fifty years later, Sohn entered Seoul's Olympic Stadium in 1988, as a national hero. Photo courtesy of the South Korean Olympic Committee Archives.

regions of the Korean Peninsula, to develop an atomic weapon during the last gasp desperation years of World War II. But after the devastating atomic blasts at Hiroshima and Nagasaki, Japan reluctantly surrendered, ending the war in the Pacific. Russian forces immediately moved into northern Korea and seized those abandoned nuclear sites, as well as petroleum processing plants, hydroelectric dams, and other heavy industries.

As Russian forces invaded the northern provinces of Korea, American troops occupied the south, with both sides agreeing to split the country along the 38th Parallel. Several years later, in an attempt to unify the two Koreas, under Communist rule, the North's native son—Kim Il Sung, who had fought against the Japanese—amassed his troops to invade the south. After three years of bitter back and forth combat, the two sides agreed to a stalemate, an armistice agreement, splitting the country along the 38th Parallel, again.

According to the official DPRK narrative, "the heroic anti-Japanese armed struggle of the Korean revolutionaries and people led by President Kim Il Sung achieved a brilliant victory, and thus Korea was liberated." (In rewriting of World War II history, the DPRK fails to mention that quite possibly it was two atomic bombs and the potential invasion of mainland Japan, which may have had a much bigger impact on the ending of the war, than anything Kim Il Sung did in Korea.)

For Sohn Kee Chung, the war had been devastating to his country and to him personally. Soon after World War II, he had become head coach of Korea's marathon team, and at the 1950 Boston Marathon, his runners swept the top three spots. But with war raging, the team returned home, to fight for their homeland. Many of the runners who trained with Sohn didn't survive the war.

Sohn continued to be an important figure in Korean sports and was a key member of the organizing community that secured the 1988 Games for Seoul.

More than five decades after his gold medal win in Berlin, the seventy-six-year-old Sohn Kee Chung carried the torch into Seoul's track and field stadium for the opening ceremony of the XXIV Olympiad, hobbled by the wear and tear of a long distance runner, but leaping for joy, proud of his Olympic victory and his country's heritage.

Four years later, at the 1992 Barcelona Games, Sohn Kee Chung watched another of his protégés—Hwang Young Jo—win Korea's second Olympic gold medal, for the marathon. Standing close by, Sohn finally heard the Korean national anthem and watched as the South Korean national flag was raised during the medals ceremony. Recalling the bitterness he felt when he had won Olympic gold for Japan more than fifty years earlier, Sohn stated, just before he died in 2002, "The Japanese could stop our musicians from playing our songs. They could stop our singers and silence our speakers, but they could not stop me from running."

The heroic story of Sohn Kee Chung—proud of his accomplishments as an athlete, prouder for his Korean heritage—is inspiring to all Koreans, young and old.

· 2 ·

DMZ Incidents

Who is the slayer, who the victim? —Sophocles

Agitate the enemy and ascertain the pattern of his movement. Determine his dispositions and so ascertain the field of battle. Probe him and learn where his strength is abundant and where deficient. —Sun Tzu, *The Art of War*

There is no occasion for celebration or boisterous conduct. We are faced with the same enemy, only a short distance away, and must be ready for any moves he makes. —General Maxwell Taylor after announcing the Armistice Agreement, July 27, 1953

The Demilitarized Zone that separates North Korea from South Korea is a 155-mile-long slash across the peninsula. It is only 2.5 miles wide with simple marker posts denoting the border between these two hostile neighbors. Calling it a "demilitarized" zone is a misnomer of great magnitude because the DMZ is one of the most heavily armed regions in the world—a powder keg just waiting for someone to light the fuse.

There have been more than forty thousand truce violations since 1953, ranging from minor fisticuffs to brutal killings, from moving heavy artillery forward to firing machine-guns, mortars, and even artillery at enemy positions within the zone since the Armistice Agreement was signed. Each time an act of provocation occurs, each side denies being the instigator.

North Korea has pursued a radical anti–American line for decades because American troops stationed in South Korea pose the greatest obstacle to its planned invasion of the south and the so-called goal of peaceful reunification. As a result North Korea has intentionally committed nearly ceaseless anti-U.S. provocations since the Korean Armistice. (Some feel that if U.S. forces were

JOURNAL

From a distance it's hard to imagine the scope and number of violations that have occurred along the DMZ, especially in the 1960s and '70s. But being there, passing through the Southern Barrier Fence with flak jacket drawn tight, heart pounding like a deafening echo, and nervously sweating (even in December), I remember wondering, hoping it would be one of the few days when no incidents flared.

Been there. Seen it. Heard it. There had been a war still going on inside the truce zone . . . along the 38th Parallel . . . and down through the western invasion corridors . . . and in the streets of Seoul . . . and on every inch of Korean coastline for more than fifty years.

The Communists' hit and run, hide and seek (chicken shit) tactics continued into the twenty-first century, though it does fluctuate as the political climate changes. Hopefully recent agreements will come to fruition and peace will finally come to the Korean Peninsula. Only time will tell.

If not I have no doubt, that if the North foolishly attempts to attack the South, the combined forces of the United States and South Korea will overwhelm and destroy the North. Without question.

Guard Post Ouellette sits only a few feet from the Military Demarcation Line separating North from South Korea. Soldiers there maintain round-the-clock monitoring of enemy activity. Photo by Gary L. Bloomfield.

pulled completely from South Korea, the provocations would stop. Others believe North Korea would immediately launch an invasion of the south.)

One of the earliest reported incidents occurred on August 1, 1954, when two American soldiers were shot and killed in the Demilitarized Zone. On March 3, 1974, twenty years later, thirty American guards were attacked and beaten by 120 North Korean guards in the Joint Security Area of PanMunJom.

In eight separate incidents in 1976, twenty-three American soldiers were murdered.

These provocations by North Korea are designed to lay the responsibility for tension in the region on the U.S. troops occupying South Korea, to mislead international opinion that the U.S. military presence is the worst threat to peace on the peninsula, and to give realistic justification for the United States to pull its troops out of the Republic.

The anti-U.S. provocations also serve to justify the tyrannical rule of Kim Il Sung (who turned over authority to his son Kim Jong Il) over the North Korean populace. Father and son had been telling their restive people that South Korea must be liberated from the U.S. belligerents—resulting in praise for anti-U.S. provocations, which were termed heroic deeds. Since Kim Jong Il passed away, his son Kim Jong Un has taken over—the first time three generations of one family have ruled a Communist country.

When a violation flares along the border zone the United Nations, American, and North and South Korean sources will issue a denial and point an accusing finger at the other side. But a closer look will reveal that virtually every clash is initiated by the North and is often met with an equal response from the U.S. and South Korean forces.

Violations were often deadly and in the 1960s and 1970s they were a constant threat to American and South Korean soldiers stationed along the DMZ as part of the United Nations Command (UNC). The zone has remained a volatile hot spot through the decades.

- On October 3, 1962, an American Army private was standing guard late at night when he was killed. "He was shot four times and stabbed eight times," reported *Stars and Stripes*. "A bayonet and two shells of the type used in Russian-made burp guns, were found near the body."
- On October 18, 1969, four 7th Infantry Division soldiers were riding in a jeep clearly displaying a white flag, when they were ambushed by North Korean soldiers. Each of the American soldiers was shot in the head and the jeep was riddled with bullet holes and grenade fragments.
- On May 3, 1977, two UNC soldiers checking a fence located about eight hundred meters south of the DMZ in the central sector of Korea, discovered a hole in the fence. As they started to investigate the hole,

In mid-April 1968, four UNC soldiers were killed when their truck was ambushed by North Korean infiltrators hiding along the road leading into the DMZ. The truck was raked with machine-gun fire. United Nations Command photo.

North Korean intruders north of the fence shot and killed one soldier and wounded another.

- On July 14, 1977, a U.S. Army Chinook helicopter was shot down after it strayed across the MDL. Three airmen were killed and one was taken prisoner.
- On December 6, 1979, an American foot patrol accidentally crossed the line during heavy fog and one soldier was killed when he stepped on a land mine. Four others were injured.
- In November 1987 an American soldier was killed, another wounded, and two North Koreans were killed during a clash across the MDL, near the Joint Security Area.
- On December 17, 1994, a U.S. Army Kiowa helicopter strayed across the MDL, ten kilometers inside North Korea and was shot down. One crewman was killed and the other taken prisoner, held for nearly two weeks.
- On the morning of July 17, 2003, North and South Korean forces along the DMZ opened fire. No injuries were reported by either side.

- On August 4, 2015, while patrolling the southern side of the MDL, two South Korean soldiers were wounded when they stepped on land mines adjacent to their guard post. The mines had been placed there by North Korean commandos. Two weeks later, South Korean forces played propaganda messages on loudspeakers directed toward the north. The same day North Korean soldiers fired a rocket and artillery shells, trying to knock out the broadcasting station. South Korean forces responded with an artillery barrage on the rocket site.

NEWS REPORTS

Local Korean news sources in the 1960s and 1970s reported DMZ incidents almost every week, in rapid-fire succession. Some of those, involving the killing or injuring of Americans and South Koreans include:

- "Two U.S. Army soldiers were killed and 18 others injured when several explosions shattered their barracks near the DMZ. The explosions were the result of North Korean Communist actions. The incidents occurred within a compound of the 2nd Infantry Division's 3rd Brigade."
- "At least three North Korean intruders were killed in a fire fight south of the Military Demarcation Line. The gunfight was the third in one week along the DMZ and was one of the worst since the 1953 Armistice."
- "Six U.S. soldiers were killed when they were attacked by a number of North Korean intruders south of the DMZ."
- "Before dawn July 16th, 1966, an unknown number of North Korean intruders killed three U.S. soldiers in the 2nd Division sector of the Armistice line."
- "Three soldiers were killed and 17 injured when North Korean soldiers ambushed a U.S. Army truck near Freedom Village inside the DMZ."
- "An undisclosed number of North Korean troops sneaked over the southern boundary of the DMZ and killed two American servicemen, one Korean soldier and wounded twenty others."

These incidents were frequent. When an incident is simply ignored, the North Koreans push a little further to see how far they can go, how much they can get away with. The only message that rings loud and clear to them is force.

As an example, the North Koreans made the mistake of attacking an isolated South Korean Army outpost along the MDL, killing the soldiers there.

Once news got out, the south (ROK) simply brought out the heavy artillery and lobbed a few shells on a North Korean guard post on the far side of the DMZ. Amazingly, there were no complaints lodged by either side, citing violations of the Armistice, and even more surprising, there were no retaliatory incidents. Eventually the zone returned to normal—if the daily killings, firefights, ambushes, and bombings could be considered anything close to normal.

The tensions began soon after the Armistice Agreement was signed in 1953.

In the early years several countries participated in joint observer team meetings and investigations of border incidents. John Dryden Sr., who served with the Royal Australian Regiment, as part of the UNC at Munsan-Ni from 1955 to 1957, recalled an exchange of gunfire that started out peacefully.

Dryden was escorting the senior Australian representative with the UNC.

I remember one particular incident that occurred on May Day of 1956. One of our allied patrols—probably American—ran smack bang into a North Korean patrol, and they were hopped up on rice wine as was often the case, and they decided to swap wine and their obligatory rice cakes with the American soldiers. All went okay until one of the communist soldiers got up as if to relieve himself in the bushes, then he spun round, pistol in hand and began firing at the UNC patrol, hitting one of the South Korean soldiers in the hip. All hell broke loose and everyone was firing their weapons. The original shooter was shot dead on the spot and everyone scattered. How more were not hit remains a mystery.

During the first shaky years of peace in Korea, both sides admitted to only a small number of "accidental" violations of the Armistice. From 1953 to 1956, for example, the North Koreans admitted to only four violations, despite staggering evidence to refute those minimal claims. After that the number of actual incidents soared, though North Korea continued to admit guilt in only a handful. There were sixty such incidents in 1957; the number rose to 1,295 by 1964. These incidents nearly doubled by 1971 to 2,483 and doubled again by 1974 to 5,415.

In 1963 two American helicopter pilots had been shot down and seized by the North Koreans while flying a routine inspection of border markings—conducted to ensure that the warning markers aren't covered up or moved by infiltrators. Charges and countercharges were exchanged in 1964 before the pilots were released. The UNC, which authorized the flights, openly admitted that the two pilots had been flying along the Han River Estuary to ensure that all military demarcation signs were visible when they inadvertently strayed across the border. Their helicopter was subsequently forced down by North Korean ground fire.

The North Koreans countered that the two pilots, Captain Ben Weakley Stutts and Captain Carleton William Voltz, had admitted to "crimes of espionage and illegal intrusion."

The statement was purportedly signed by an American Air Force major general, who at the time served as senior member of the Military Armistice Commission for the UNC at PanMunJom.

But the newspaper *Korean Republic* reported on May 17, 1964, that "Colonel Paul Hinkley, UNC representative, denied the Communist allegation, saying 'all the records clearly show that they, (the two pilots) were not engaged in espionage activities.'"

The mid- to late 1960s were especially dangerous for GIs and their ROK colleagues stationed along the DMZ. Some attribute the escalation of true violations to Kim Il Sung's son—Kim Jong Il—wanting to prove himself as an eventual successor to his father. Others viewed it as a coordinated effort with communist forces in Vietnam, who hoped to redeploy South Korean units back to their homeland to repel the escalating threat. In Vietnam three divisions of South Korean soldiers had deployed in support of American troops. Known for their toughness, these ROK forces quickly earned a reputation for their brutal tactics, and Vietnamese and Viet Cong units steered clear of them whenever possible. As the war in Vietnam escalated near the end of 1967, Pyongyang promptly increased activity all along the DMZ.

Beginning in November 1966, more than two dozen Americans were killed and scores more were wounded in combat along the DMZ. Artillery fire was used by ROK troops in April 1967 to repel a communist incursion in a battle that involved more than one hundred men. In June of that year, a U.S. 2nd Infantry Division barracks was dynamited. September saw two South Korean trains blasted, one carrying U.S. military supplies. In October, North Korean artillery fire sounded for the first time since 1953 when more than fifty rounds were fired at a South Korean army barracks.

One such incident in the late 1960s was dramatically featured in a report by Major Vandon Jenerette, titled "The Forgotten DMZ":

> The point man gripped his M16 rifle tightly as he pushed through the underbrush. Carefully looking for booby traps along the trail, he strained his ears listening for the slightest sound to his front. It was dark as the patrol inched its way forward through the valley far below the guard posts on the hills of the demilitarized zone (DMZ). A branch snapped somewhere in the darkness. The point man turned to signal the patrol to stop as a shot rang out, hitting him in the chest. Grenades exploded, sending blinding flashes along with shrapnel into the night sky in all directions.
>
> The young sergeant leading the patrol ran forward in a low crouch as his men automatically started shooting and fanned out along the sides of

the trail. As he crested the small rise separating the main body from the point man, a burst of fire caught him in the shoulder, knocking him to the ground. He fought to remain conscious as he crawled toward the body of the point man. He yelled, but there was no answer.

Meanwhile, as the radio operator grabbed the hand mike of the radio and called back to the command post for help, the assistant patrol leader shouted for covering fire and slithered forward. Everyone was shooting, and the dull 'thunk' of the M79 grenade launcher was answered by a 'kaboom' as it exploded on the far side of the rise. The sergeant's voice could be heard between the shooting as he yelled for a medic, and the specialist four, now in charge, had only one thing on his mind—to get the wounded out of the line of fire. He shouted back to the men in the rear to move around the hill to a position where they could put more fire on the enemy; but as quickly as it had begun, the shooting stopped.

Another serious incident occurred in August 1967 when GIs waiting outside a mess tent were cut down by a barrage of bullets. The incident was reported in *Pacific Stars and Stripes*:

Communist machine-gun fire suddenly burst upon American and South Korean soldiers Monday. They had just returned from their day's engineering work and were forming a chow line for dinner outside a mess hall near the Demilitarized Zone on Korea's western front. Others were caught inside the mess hall tents waiting to be served. An estimated 3,000 rounds of machine-gun and other automatic weapons fire were poured into the area. The attack left three soldiers dead, one American and two South Koreans and 28 others including 14 American soldiers wounded.

U.S. Navy Lt. Commander George McMichael pointed out blood pools outside and inside the mess hall tents which were riddled with hundreds of Communist bullets. He said that the fire came some 250 yards away from a 105-foot high hill overlooking the compound in a valley. Two of the 14 wounded Americans were members of the Quick Reaction Force. They were wounded from the explosion of a land mine on a road leading to the Communist gun positions. Over 1,000 rounds of Soviet 7.62mm ammunition were found at the Communist positions, the UN Command said. McMichael said that the mine was believed to have been planted by the Communist infiltrators. He estimated that 9 to 12 North Koreans were involved in the raid but could not tell whether they were regular North Korean soldiers or saboteurs.

With the escalation of incidents, the U.S. and South Korean forces responded by reinforcing the guard posts and observation posts inside and near the DMZ, and spraying defoliants to reduce brush and tall grasses

JOURNAL

I'm not sure why our guys up there feel any obligation to play by the rules. Them other guys sure don't. If you're in a back alley brawl with thugs who don't believe in the Marquis of Queensberry Rules of Boxing, you can't proceed to fight in a civilized manner and still hope they don't just beat the holy crap out of you. That's what they're counting on. Personally, I prefer one of the Abstract Rules of Combat, which I can't remember word for word, but this is close enough:
"In every battle, as well as in chess, the ultimate victor is the one who makes the next to last mistake."

where enemy soldiers could hide and wait to ambush a foot patrol or passing vehicle.

These measures markedly increased the number of reported contacts, though at the same time North Korean penetrations dropped off. North Koreans began to fall victim to ambushes and suffer from chance encounters with alerted (UNC) troops.

THE OFFICIAL REPORTS OF DMZ ACTIVITY

In its Annual Historical Supplement, the 3rd Brigade of the 2nd Infantry Division filed the following, in February 1968:

> The Third Brigade, northernmost America military unit in Korea, stands guard over an 18 & a half-mile section of the DMZ. The Brigade's mission is to provide continual surveillance over its sector of the zone and vigilantly guard against any hostile North Korean acts or efforts by North Korean agents to infiltrate through the Brigade's area of responsibility. From May to September (1967), combat with the North Koreans became a daily occurrence to the men of the Third Brigade. In this five-month period, Third Brigade soldiers engaged infiltrators on 264 separate occasions with counter intrusion fire. In addition, there were 47 firefights between North Koreans and Third Brigade soldiers, three minings in the Brigade sector, and one raid carried out by ten North Koreans on a Third Brigade compound. The raid by North Koreans on 22 July against Camp Walley on the right flank of the Brigade sector was probably the most serious of numerous incidents during this period. In this raid, two barracks were blown up by satchel charges, with heavy loss of life and limb among the occupants.

The 2nd Battalion of the 23rd Infantry further noted in its February of 1968 report:

It was during the last week of [April] that three C Company GIs and one KATUSA were occupying a night stake-out position on the DMZ, when a group of North Korean infiltrators approached the rear of their position. (The GIs) opened fire on the agents. Three North Korean agents were killed and another one possibly seriously wounded. It was on 17 July 1967, that a group of North Korean infiltrators attacked and overran a Bravo Company position on the DMZ using automatic weapons and hand grenades. Three American soldiers were killed and one KATUSA wounded. The morning after the attack, Bravo Company began a chase that brought them to the Military Demarcation Line of the DMZ, where they were brought under fire with heavy machine-guns from North Korea and pinned down for approximately an hour and a half. It was during the sweep in pursuit of the North Koreans, that (one of our soldiers) shot and killed one of the agents with a .45 (caliber) pistol. An American sergeant was also wounded during this same sweep action.

In the Department of Defense, "Report of the 1971 Quadrennial Review it was reported that during the period of May 1967 to January 1968, there were more than 300 hostile acts in the U.S. sector of the DMZ, resulting in fifteen American soldiers killed and another 65 wounded."

In October 1968 the 2nd Infantry Division's Operation Report on DMZ actions noted an increase in enemy activity: "The number of attempted penetrations of the Barrier Fence increased from one during the previous reporting period to seven this period. There were also more attempted penetrations of the DMZ via the Imjin River than previously experienced. (North Korean) agent teams became involved in an increasing number of firefights with friendly patrols and security forces in the DMZ (15 firefights last period; 46 firefights this period) and harassment of barrier positions at night increased significantly. Analysis of DMZ incidents indicated that an increased number of short-range reconnaissance teams were being dispatched to the 2nd Infantry Division sector. Breaching of the Barrier was accomplished by cutting through and digging under the fence at night. Some teams bypassed the barrier by entering the Imjin River from the (North Korean) side and floating with the current into the Division sector. There were no significant changes in the type of equipment carried by the intruders and tactics employed remained essentially the same. When compromised, the enemy chose to run; when in danger of capture, he chose suicide."

To understand the mindset of the North Korean soldiers assigned to the DMZ, Ju Sung Hil—a former enemy soldier explained: "On the DMZ, everyone is considered the enemy. We have to kill without question." That shoot to kill order included any North Korean residents or soldiers who might attempt to defect to the south. (Despite those dangers, Ju Sung Hil in fact defected, navigating through a minefield, at night, and penetrating an electrified fence, surrendering at a South Korean guard post positioned along the MDL.) "I personally believe that I made it through with guidance of an invisible hand, because of God's will."

Tragically, Ju's actions were not without consequences. Once word of his defection was reported, his family was imprisoned and may have been executed.

TWO SIDES OF THE STORY

One example of conflicting news reporting focused on President Lyndon Johnson's 1968 visit to South Korea and the DMZ.

The *New York Times* reported:

> On April 15, 1968, two Americans died when their truck was ambushed and machine-gunned near Pyongyang shortly after President Lyndon Johnson had inspected the area.

The article went on to say that in that one year alone there had been more than 350 shootings across the line, resulting in 500 killed.

That's 500 men killed in one year alone.

A more detailed report of the incident, titled "Survivors Seen Lucky to Be Alive" was released by *Stars and Stripes* two days later:

> Observers at the scene of Sunday's bold ambush by Communist North Koreans who machine-gunned and killed four United Nations Command soldiers reached one conclusion: "I don't see how anybody survived this." About 20 bullet holes could be seen in the shattered front windshield of the truck. Both headlights were blasted out. Three of the tires were punctured and at least 40 rounds had ripped through the truck's rear canvas cover. Two UNC troops survived the attack, but were wounded. A pool of dried blood, a severed wristwatch, glass fragments and discarded bandage wrappers were scattered around the ground near the truck.

Army Specialist 4 Leroy Jacks was one of those survivors:

> I had written my mother that "it's been too quiet here lately," just the day before. It was last Easter Sunday, about eleven at night. We were in a ¾-ton truck, six of us, going north in the DMZ to our guard post in the Joint Security Area. We were driving along, singing country music, when

a grenade hit the right front wheel of the truck and stopped us. Then I saw muzzle flashes from both sides of the road—maybe 10 men in three firing positions just 10 to 20 feet ahead of us. I was hit in the leg and got down and doubled up on the floor of the truck. Sergeant (James) Anderson started to get out of the truck, yelling, "O.K. you got us, we surrender." There was a burst of automatic weapons fire, and he fell dead on top of me. Then they came up to the truck and started rummaging around. I felt somebody jerk the .45 pistol from my holster. I was trying to freeze, but I was so scared my left leg kept fluttering.

Jacks survived the ambush by feigning his death. Before leaving the scene, the North Koreans raked the back of the truck with bullets, then scattered.

One other soldier survived the attack—Private David Bibee, who had only been in country for less than a month.

"We just didn't have a chance," he said. "They seemed to come from behind. The only thing I could make out was that there were at least six of them. They caught us off guard. The first thing I knew a hand grenade hit right beside me. I was blown airborne, some 40 feet down the side of the hill we were on. I was shocked and dazed by the blast of the grenade, and then I heard more grenades going off, and automatic weapons were firing all around with the chatter of burp guns. The only reason I'm alive now is because I didn't move when a North Korean yanked my watch off my wrist—I played dead. I didn't reckon it lasted more than 15 or 20 minutes."

Despite being wounded by forty-eight grenade fragments, Bibee was able to wave down an approaching Army truck, and when the driver asked what happened, Bibee said "they're all dead," without knowing Specialist Jacks had also survived.

From the northern side of the DMZ, Wilfred G. Burchett (an Australian reporter and North Korean sympathizer who wrote frequently about supposed-American transgressions) spun the same incident differently. Kim Il Sung felt that during his visit to the border area, President Johnson told his soldiers to instigate more border flare-ups.

"Since that visit the Americans have greatly stepped up their military provocations in and around the Demilitarized Zone," Burchett reported.

In March 1969, a ten-man work party was replacing some of the markers along the Military Demarcation Line when North Korean soldiers in a nearby guard post opened fire. Eight American soldiers and an ROK soldier were killed.

According to a report in *Stars and Stripes*, "the work party was pinned down by machine-gun and small arms fire without warning, and a UNC patrol in the area moved to assist, but was also pinned down. One man was killed by the fire, and three others were wounded. The spokesman said it was not immediately known whether the casualties were Americans or South Koreans. Both have forces in the buffer strip. The other deaths came when a U.S. Army helicopter evacuating the three wounded men crashed at 9:45 p.m. near the zone, killing all passengers—the three wounded, and five other crewmen."

FABRICATIONS BECOME "TRUTH"

In the mid-1970s the provocations were endless. The *Korea Herald* wrote on August 21, 1976: "The Pyongyang side has considerably expanded its offense capability by introducing to the western frontline missile bases and highly sophisticated landing craft."

Kim Il Sung, during a 1976 talk with a Japanese newspaper editor, declared his innocence in border clashes with the South, saying, "Who will believe that such a small country as ours is threatening the United States, that is seeking to dominate the world? No people in the world believe it. And yet the U.S. imperialists and the South Korean authorities persist in their unfounded argument that we are threatening South Korea. Quite contrary is the fact, not we but precisely the U.S. imperialists and the South Korean authorities are creating the danger of war; we are not threatening South Korea. The U.S. imperialists are threatening us."

Less than a year later, on May 15, 1977, the *Korea Times* reported, "Two North Korean spy boats fired on a South Korean ship off the south coast." An article in Korea *News Review* magazine stated in August 1977 that "bellicose North Korean Communists, who have never changed their basic policy to communize the south by force, have made ceaseless provocations against the south."

Countering, a North Korean general issued a statement saying, "Where the Americans have accused us of violations they have never produced an iota of proof. We have never had to admit any violations. We have never sent any ships into their waters nor planes into their air space. We have never introduced heavy weapons into the DMZ."

Typical noncommittal North Korean replies to United Nations accusations of an Armistice violation include: "Our side knows of no such violation," or "It is a frame-up by your side," or "We will look into the cases."

Rarely, since the Armistice, has any member of the Communist delegation to PanMunJom admitted wrongdoing or even the slightest culpability in a border clash. In their eyes, each violation is just "another piece in the American warmonger's provocative strategy to resuming hostilities between Korean brothers."

But while it's easy to take sides with the "good guys" and denounce North Korean statements as propaganda, it is hard to ignore some of the statistics they've compiled, distorted or not, and put on display for North Koreans and foreign tourists, portraying Americans as "blood-thirsty warmongers."

Burchett, the pro-North Korean reporter, wrote that on April 5, 1967, American and south Korean soldiers fired across the border, killing six North Korean security guards. "The slain Koreans were killed by a heavy machine-gun, the introduction of which into the DMZ is in itself a serious violation."

On the southern side of the fence, this same story was run by a South Korean wire service and printed in local newspapers, stating simply, "On April 5, four North Koreans were killed in the Demilitarized Zone." The North logged a complaint at Pyongyang but nothing more was said about why the killings occurred, or which side actually started it.

MANIPULATING THE NEWS

And a North Korean military official, trying to add further credence to President Kim's comment, reflected on numerous other "attempts to harm or destroy" North Korea along the DMZ and in coastal waters that took place in early November 1968, supposedly all initiated by U.S. and/or South Korean forces.

> On November 3rd, along the western part of the Demarcation Line, [South Korean] troops, after firing red signal flares, and covered by heavy machine-gun fire, swarmed across the Demarcation Line and attacked our positions with hand grenades and rifles. Similar incidents occurred on November 4th and 5th. On November 4th, an enemy gunboat penetrated some four miles into our East Sea waters and stayed there for four hours. On November 5th, submarine chasers also penetrated our coastal areas, and on November 22nd, after a U.S. reconnaissance plane had been over, three U.S. naval vessels again intruded into our waters and bombarded our coast.

Near-verbatim statements are issued by the South Korean government, claiming self-defense and denouncing North Korean attacks:

- "A group of 31 North Korean commandos infiltrated Seoul and killed many persons by throwing hand grenades and firing indiscriminately. The intruders threw hand grenades at a passing bus and killed six people."

- "North Korea has built underground invasion tunnels south of the Military Demarcation Line in an apparent attempt to infiltrate into the south."
- "Two U.S. Army helicopters flying southeast of the Han and Imjin rivers were fired upon from the North Korean side."
- "A North Korean Army guard post machine-gunned a United Nations Command observation post across the Military Demarcation Line."

TATTLING ON THE OTHER GUY

These incidents, as with other acts of provocation instigated by North Korean, UN, U.S., or South Korean forces, are promptly reported to the Military Armistice Commission at PanMunJom, then forwarded to the UN Security Council for the world arena to report on. Each incident is thus reported to and entered in the record of the UN Security Council, but little else is done to curb further provocations.

Rarely do the Council members even agree on which side is the perpetrator in an incident—the American and South Korean "imperialists" or the North Korean "belligerents." It all depends on where each delegate's allegiance is.

So in the eyes of the world, who is right and who is wrong? Or is it a seesaw battle as each side waits to catch the other off-guard?

More than 1,200 American, South Korean, and North Korean soldiers have died along the DMZ in the past six decades. They could probably say who to point the finger at, but then again, it would only be their word against everyone else. The actual number of Americans killed is hard to pin down because some DMZ incidents have been conveniently listed as "training accidents."

Captain Jonathan Stafford, in his paper "Finding America's Role in a Collapsed North Korean State" for *Military Review*'s January/February 2008 issue wrote:

> North Korea has been a U.S. adversary responsible for the deaths of thousands of American service members over the past 55 years. . . . During the 55 years since the end of the Korean War, the United States has kept troops in South Korea to maintain the UN-brokered armistice that ended the conflict. Over 36,000 American Soldiers died during the Korean War. North Korea has killed more than 750 others since the signing of the armistice.

(The exact number of American soldiers killed after the Armistice is questionable. Some sources say the number is less than 100. The above source said thousands. The figure most often used is more than 1,200, but this includes American and North and South Korean forces.)

Battle doesn't determine who is right . . . only who is left. —Peter Bowman

If we're killed on a patrol or a guard post, crushed in a jeep accident or shot by a nervous GI on the fence, no one will ever write about us . . . or erect a monument or read a Gettysburg Address over our graves. We'll never be part of the national memory. —William Hollinger, *The Fence Walker*

JOURNAL: 355 DAYS LEFT

Went to the DMZ today for the first time. Tied a white flag on our jeep. Flak jacket weighs a ton and has a hole in the material and a small dent in the back. I have to wonder if it's from a bullet, or if the armorer took a ball peen hammer and pounded it.

Asked the unit armorer for a .45 instead of an M-16, which is ridiculous to fuss with when I also have two cameras and a bag full of lenses and film and batteries.

On the drive up to the DMZ I checked my ammo clip and there was only one bullet. What the hell am I supposed to do with ONE BULLET!?

Got to the Southern Barrier Fence and the MP told us to load our weapons because North Korean infiltrators were suspected in the area. So if we get ambushed do I use that one bullet on them? Or me? Couldn't help but laugh, thinking of one of the Abstract Rules of Combat:

"When in danger or in doubt, run in circles, scream and shout."

Before leaving, I decided to write a letter to my wife and daughter, just in case—

Dear Anita,

Getting my gear ready to go into the DMZ for the first time. There hasn't been any incidents lately, but we just never know. Probably nothing will happen, but figure I'd better write, just in case. And if I make it back, I'll just throw it away.

So anyway, if you're reading this, it means I'm no longer among the living. One of my room mates or co-workers will be sending all my stuff home, including this letter, which I'm leaving on my bunk. Take care of Angie. I wish I could see into the future, and see what a wonderful young lady she'll become. Remind her of me now and then, and let her know I'll be watching over her. And please don't mourn me for the rest of your life. You've got so much love to give. You deserve to be happy.

Love always.

Author's Note: I went to the DMZ sixteen times and wrote sixteen letters. Fortunately my wife never got any of them.

JOURNAL

Talked with a squad of 11 Bang-Bangs while on the DMZ. They asked if I had heard about the death of one of their friends. I hadn't. They gave me his name and how he died—throat slit while on guard duty—and wanted me to see what the official report said. Came back to Division HQ and asked a friend of mine who works in the Tactical Operations Center to check it out. He got back with me later that night, said the death was reported simply as a "training accident."

A week later I made it back to the Z, and sought out any of the guys in the squad from before. Two of them were sacked out. The others were out on patrol and wouldn't be back before I had to catch a helicopter flight back to Camp Casey. I woke up the two, who remembered me, and I told them about the "training accident." They tossed out a string of curse words then went back to sleep.

I had some time to kill before my ride, so I went to the ready room where some guys were playing cards. They'd seen me a few times before and knew I either wanted to ask them something or maybe shoot some photos. This time it was questions.

I asked how they felt about the North Korean infiltrators probing the DMZ for weaknesses, for opportunities:

"They usually harasses the ROK Army soldiers, because if they mess with us Americans it'll start an international incident like the Tree Massacre a year ago. Every once-in-a-while he tests us though to see how far we can be pushed," commented soldiers from the 2nd Infantry Division's 1/31st Infantry Battalion on temporary duty near the DMZ.

"After a few months up here the daily incidents don't bother us anymore. We become immune . . . shell-shocked. Usually we joke about it, and sometimes on payday we'll take bets on who's gonna die next, or which patrol is going to get ambushed. And nobody wants to get stuck with one of the new guys cause they go out there jabbering constantly, and clattering their gear, attracting all sorts of attention. Bad Ju-Ju just having them with us. We keep plenty of distance from them when we're outside the wire."

"Maybe our sense of humor is a little warped, but laughing at death is easier than running from it. Besides, the only guys who really get paranoid are the married dudes. That could be because we call Joe Chink 'the Widow Maker.' The guys who are getting short, especially when they're under 30 days till they head back to the states, they get a little twitchy too."

The lookout shack at Guard Post Ouellette—situated only a few yards from the Military Demarcation Line—is a great vantage point to keep an eye out for enemy infiltrators. Photo by Gary L. Bloomfield.

AN ELEVEN BANG BANG REMEMBERS DUTY ON THE Z

Army Specialist 4 Geoffrey Porter served with the 1st Battalion, 38th Infantry, 2nd Infantry Division: "I was young back then, I think we all were. It was the mid '70s and I didn't realize how extraordinary the circumstances were that put me there. Our leadership had indoctrinated us all very well about just who and what we faced across the fence. We were at the ass-end of the longest supply chain in the world, armed to the teeth but were just a few companies of troops, however well-trained we may have been.

"The North Koreans would periodically harass our compound or provoke incidents, with Americans when possible, in an attempt to keep us unsure and off balance. Our compound was called Four-Papa-One, a collection of sandbag bunkers that faced the DMZ. What we were was a speed bump if the North decided to come south.

"All these years later it seems peculiar what I remember so clearly. I was an Eleven-B Spec-4 on my third year in the Army, five months into my tour in Korea. Veterans of that time period may recall AFKN, or the Armed Forces

Korea Network radio stations on AM. It was a hot early morning at about 6 a.m. exactly and the radio was playing the Charlie Tuna Show on my little pocket transistor radio. He always opened his morning show with the song 'Good Morning Starshine.'

"I was sitting on the roof of this 4-man bunker eating a C-Ration. Remember beans and meatballs? Cold? That was a taste I'll never forget and don't want to remember. I was wearing fatigue pants, boots, a T-shirt, my web gear and my helmet (Steel Pot) with my M16 on my lap as I ate, always watching for enemy activity. I remember wondering what my friends back home would think of my adventure."

Forty years after leaving Korea, Porter still has vivid memories of his time on the Z.

JOURNAL: 162 DAYS LEFT

Time stops at the southern bank of the Imjin River where Freedom Bridge stands like a gateway to hell. The surrounding tank traps, and concrete bunkers, and concertina wire, and minefields. It's a state of war, just waiting for someone to make the wrong move.

And when it happens several hundred American soldiers caught in the middle are expected to die in that initial volley. That's not a prediction, or prophesy, rumor, or speculation. One full infantry battalion with battle streamers flying will die along the northern bank of the Imjin.

Freedom Bridge is a locked-in target for both the North and South Korean armies. North Korean artillery will destroy it to trap the Z battalion for easy pickings. The ROK Army will detonate the nearby tank traps to stall the enemy advance. Why worry about a few hundred American soldiers caught on the wrong side of the river?

The lump in the throat and the butterflies in the stomach don't go away until we're back on the Imjin's southern shore.

• 3 •

The Minefield

Talking of thousands of soldiers dying or being wounded would make an audience shake its head or cluck its tongue in horror, but they really didn't feel it. But if one soldier could be descriptively isolated and made identifiable as an individual, so that in a few brief strokes the audience got to "see" and like him, and then they were told that this boy's legs were cut off by a shrapnel burst, the emotional impact was heightened by identification with the victim. —Louis Nizer

Radar Site #4 sits on a lonely hilltop near the DMZ, overlooking the truce village of PanMunJom to the west, Camp Liberty Bell at the base of the hill's southern slope, and due north "you can see the end of the world."

It's not a very impressive setting—just a long building where the radars keep watch on friendly ground patrols and enemy infiltrators in the area, surrounded by a blanket of sand that covers the hill a few yards further than the compound's barbed wire perimeter fence.

And although RS4 is well south of the Demilitarized Zone, it still offers an unobstructed view of Communist North Korea just off in the distance. Being newly assigned there as a "watch," a young American soldier recalled his first day at the site, in the mid-1970s, which opened his eyes to the goings-on of the DMZ, and "made me realize that after all these years there's still a war going on in Korea."

At the time he was only nineteen, fresh out of high school, hoping to be assigned to an army post close to home "because I've never been out of the states. Now look where I am. The other guys call this the edge of the world. I couldn't even point out Korea on a map.

"When I first got here the only thing that really grabbed my attention was that sign over there," the private remarked while pointing to a white wood

Every guard post and lookout point on the DMZ faces north—where the end of the world exists. Photo by Gary L. Bloomfield.

slat sign near the perimeter fence on the northern side of the compound. It said simply, 'This is not the end of the world, but you can see it from here.'

"Naturally I was curious to see this end of the world off in the distance," the young soldier recalled, "so I walked over to the barbed wire for a better view. Because I was new to the Z, I didn't know nothing and wondered why this hilltop and every military compound in the area was covered with sand. I wondered even more about why that sand was raked into a striped pattern. I soon found out. As I walked closer to the perimeter fence, someone behind me shouted, 'STOP RIGHT WHERE YOU ARE!' I turned around to see a chunky sergeant growling at me from the doorway entrance.

"'Private,'" he bellowed sarcastically, "you just messed up my pretty sand and I don't like that. I should make you rake it real pretty like it was. Now get your ass back here, and don't make no more foot prints in my sand . . . you walk backwards . . . if you want to live another five minutes you'd better retrace your steps exactly."

"Why the big deal over raked sand," I wondered as I followed my tracks back to the building, but before I could ask the question, the sergeant had stomped off in a huff, muttering under his breath, "These young smart asses come up here and do their god-damnedest to get killed."

"Okay so what did I do that was so wrong? . . . foul up the radar some-how? . . . walk outside without my helmet and flak jacket on? Heaven forbid I should mess up his pretty rows of raked sand.

"Later on that day I had a chance to talk to one of the other privates who'd been on the Z for a few months. He took the time to spell out the facts of life up here to me. The sand is raked every morning and every night. Prior to that we check for footprints to see if Joe Chink (a North Korean infiltrator) has been snooping around. Two weeks ago a Chinese land mine was discovered in the area where I walked today. Joe Chink had probably snuck close the night before via one of his underground tunnels and buried the mine, then he raked the sand. Unfortunately it was discovered exactly the way it was intended . . . an American soldier, checking the sand, stepped on it.

"He lived, but he'll never walk again. Joe Chink's practical joke tore both his legs to shreds. Don't need to be told twice no more why they keep the sand raked."

By then the sergeant had returned. Overhearing the conversation he added, this time with a slight trace of sincerity, "Say your prayers every night, Kid and don't touch the Claymore trigger switches."

"I didn't have to wonder what he was talking about that time."

"When I die I'll go to heaven because I've spent my time in hell . . . the Demilitarized Zone of South Korea"—a popular phrase among American soldiers stationed on the DMZ.

Dennis Urban, who served with the 1st of the 9th Infantry Battalion recalled an even more perilous incident involving those deadly Claymore mines:

"The incident took place the first night I was on barrier fence duty. I was on position #128 . . . the road gate going out to PanMunJom . . . and had a sergeant training me that night. I had already been on Guard Post Katie for a few nights, then two patrols of thirty hours each. Now it was eighteen hours overnight on the fence. Before dark, we opened the gate, went out and pulled a long sawhorse barricade covered with rows of concertina wire across the narrow road, which at that time, in 1968, wasn't very wide and was made of

JOURNAL

Okay yeah, I admit it. I trampled all through the neatly raked sand, just like the newbie private. I did it the first time I visited Guard Post Ouellette, looking for good angles to shoot photos. How was I supposed to know? It was my first time up to the DMZ and nobody told us about all the precautions. I'd never really taken it too seriously before that anyway. Call it a rookie mistake, just a dumb-ass photo-journalist I are! That's why they gave me a camera instead of an M-16 to shoot with. And one bullet.

Thought of one of those Abstract Rules of Combat that seems appropriate—"No matter how intense the battle, a commander must, at all costs, avoid stepping in anything soft or sticky . . . " (or anything that might ruin your day).

dirt and mud . . . full of holes everywhere! (The perimeter fence had bells or tin cans filled with pebbles, used as warning alerts if anyone tried to penetrate our position.)

"Once we placed the barricade, we very carefully placed two Claymore mines inside the wire on the road, and also placed two trip flares inside the wire nearby. Then we withdrew and locked the gate. The wire from the Claymores led back to our foxhole position. The sergeant very carefully showed me how to secure the wire (at the end of which was a blasting cap inside the Claymore mine) into the 'clicker' device, that when squeezed quickly, created an electrical charge which went down the wire and set off the blasting cap, which then set off the Claymore mine! (When the Claymore mine is detonated, thousands of ball bearings devastate the area up to 250 meters out, shredding anything and anyone in the blast zone.)

"The sergeant carefully explained not to touch the clicker unless and until I planned to set off the mine itself. A charge can build up inside the clicker if it's played with too much (soldiers do tend to click it a lot when they are nervous). Next he explained that the North Koreans will sneak up to the barricade, carefully turn the Claymore mine around to face our position, then attach a fish hook with lots of string to the concertina wire and crawl away a hundred feet or so and off the road. Once they are in position, they pull the string, making the beer cans with pebbles in them rattle, hoping we would grab the clicker and plug it in and squeeze the trigger!!! BOOM!!! The blast would have taken us out, and they crawl away, satisfied with their dirty work.

"When they had done their work and pulled the string, it rattled the fence and I immediately jumped for the clicker just as the sergeant jumped on me!! Instead of blowing the Claymores (and killing ourselves), we fired off a half dozen M-79 grenade rounds where we thought they might be hiding. Next morning, we went out and found the turned Claymores and the fish string. Lesson learned.

"The Claymore mines being switched was something that was done all over the Z, from the barrier fence, to patrols, to the guard post positions. Many soldiers have reported accounts similar to mine. Very few Claymores were actually blown because of this. Some people who had nerves of steel would rig up a hand grenade with the pin partially removed or a trip flare with the pin partially removed to the base of the Claymore mine. They used a very, very fine wire that could not be seen, especially in the dark. Then when the mine moved, the grenade or the flare would go off!!! Boom . . . so did the Claymore! I'm sure in time the North Koreans figured out what we were doing. But it worked fine in 1968."

· *4* ·

The Tree Incident

Do not remove a fly from your friend's head with a hatchet.
—Chinese proverb

*F*or most Americans, August 18, 1976, is just another day. What they don't realize is that on that day the United States almost went to war, and it could very well have escalated to World War III—and all because of a faraway tree that had a little too much foliage.

What started out as a simple pruning by a few South Korean workers soon exploded into an international incident that pitted the overwhelming arsenal of the United States and South Korea against the maniacal Communist North Korea. And at the center of all the battle preparations stood a lonely poplar—its branches had obscured the view of Joint Security guards at PanMunJom watching North Korean activity along the DMZ, and so it needed to be trimmed.

Three days later the tree was not only trimmed, but reduced to kindling.

"North Korean guards had warned a United Nations Command team against cutting down the tree in the DMZ twelve days before the incident that led to the slaying of two Americans," testified Arthur W. Hummel Jr., assistant secretary of state, and Morton I. Abramowitz, former deputy assistant secretary of defense, before two subcommittees of the House International Relations Committee.

"According to the account of the two officials, a UN work team went to the tree August 6 for the purpose of felling it in order to improve the line of sight between two UN Command posts. North Korean guards told them to leave the tree alone. The men complied because of the Communist show of force in the area. By August 18 it had been decided to trim the tree instead of chopping it down. Nevertheless the Americans were worried about it [the operation] . . . it was a concern obviously."

On June 30, 1975, Major William Henderson, commander of the security troops at the Joint Security Area in PanMunJom was knocked to the ground and stomped on by a North Korean guard. In a similar incident, a young American lieutenant was kicked in the groin by a North Korean guard. That guard—Sergeant Pak Chol—was promoted to lieutenant for his actions. In August 1976, Pak Chol would instigate a much deadlier incident. United Nations Command photo.

There were no other events or minor clashes during the days leading up to the incident that could have provoked what took place that bloody day of August 18, 1976. It just happened, suddenly, without warning . . . deadly.

NORTH KOREAN SERGEANT PAK CHOL . . . OVERNIGHT "HERO"

Only two confrontations, several months forgotten, could be linked to the Tree Incident.

An American officer, a young lieutenant, was hunched over due to the bitter cold as he walked through the Joint Security Area. At the time both North Korean guards and UN personnel had free range, so they often came in close contact, though rarely exchanged words. But on that day, North Korean

Sergeant Pak Chol kicked the American officer in the groin, and left him in a heap, in the snow. In June 1975, Pak Chol attacked the commander of the security forces at the Joint Security Area—Major William Henderson—then stomped on him. This incident was witnessed and photographed. Soon after, Pak Chol showed up in the JSA area as a lieutenant.

On August 18, 1976, Lieutenant Pak Chol and seven other People's Army soldiers noticed the UN work party near the Bridge of No Return in the Joint Security Area and went over to watch the goings on.

"The vegetation that covers the JSA has been routinely and periodically cleared by both sides without incident," wrote Marine Colonel Conrad De-Lateur for the State Department's Foreign Service Institute, in March 1987. "Therefore, pruning the foliage of a 40-foot Normandy poplar tree in the JSA near the Bridge of No Return that obstructed the line-of-sight view between UNC Checkpoint 3 and UNC Observation Post 5 was not considered a significant or provocative event."

Two U.S. officers—Captain Arthur G. Bonifas and Lieutenant Mark T. Barrett and ROK Army Captain Kim Moon Hwan—led the group of five Korean Service Corps maintenance men and ten UNC security personnel sent out to trim the tree, which sat between a UN observation post and a North Korean post at PanMunJom.

It was a quiet summer day inside the truce village. Even North Korean Lieutenant Pak and cohorts seemed to be in a surprisingly good mood—a sharp contrast to their usual spiteful antics. When asked what was going on, Bonifas and Barrett pointed out the necessity of trimming the foliage. Pak merely replied "Good," then sat down nearby to watch.

After a few minutes though Pak suddenly jumped up and ordered the trimming stopped. The South Korean laborers understood Pak and stopped and waited for further guidance. When Bonifas countermanded the order, Pak spoke to ROK Army Captain Kim, saying, "if you cut more branches, there will be a big problem." Pak then sent one of his subordinates back across the Bridge of No Return into the North Korean sector of the JSA, returning a few minutes later with a truckload of Communist soldiers, and some from nearby guard posts, bringing the total to thirty. Pak then removed his watch, wrapped it in a handkerchief, and deposited the small bundle in his pocket.

THE DEADLY AMBUSH

Sensing what was about to occur, another North Korean soldier rolled up his sleeves, while the others mingled about, waiting, smiling like hungry tomcats toying with a cornered mouse.

"Lt. Pak threatened death if the work was not halted. The KSC laborers ceased work but Capt. Bonifas ordered the pruning to resume, confiding to Capt. Kim he believed these were only threats and that the NK guards were not intending to act," noted Colonel DeLateur. "Capt. Bonifas then turned to observe the workers and failed to see Lt. Pak taking off his watch and the other KPA officer rolling up his sleeves. A UNC guard vainly tried to warn his commander of these sinister movements, just before Lt. Pak yelled 'Chookyo (kill),' and kicked Capt. Bonifas in the groin."

Bonifas and Barrett were the first to fall, beaten unconscious immediately as the North Koreans singled them out. (Even though a small contingency of American soldiers armed with .45 caliber pistols accompanied the two slain officers, they could not unholster or fire their weapons because of a provision that governs the activity of JSA guards. Under that provision, no side arms could be drawn and fired without orders from a commissioned officer—Bonifas or Barrett in this instance—both of whom were attacked and silenced before they could issue such an order. This left the highly disciplined

It started as the simple trimming of a poplar tree that obscured the view between sentry posts inside the Joint Security Area. But when a North Korean officer ordered the trimming stopped and his demand was ignored, he promptly ordered his fellow guards to kill them. They quickly pounced on the two American officers, bludgeoning them to death with pikes and axes. United Nations Command photo.

American guards defenseless and all they could do was ward off the blows and seek safe haven.)

With the two American officers lying at their feet like sacrificial lambs, the North Koreans unleashed their fervent hatred toward all U.S. "imperialists." Axes dropped by the frightened South Korean maintenance workers were quickly picked up by the Communists and used to crush the skulls of the two unconscious American officers. Deadly blows repeatedly pulverized the lifeless bodies.

Satisfied with their handiwork, the North Korean soldiers, led by Lieutenant Pak Chol departed the area, confident that President Kim Il Sung, after hearing of the incident, would bestow full hero's honors on each of them.

Beneath the shade of that lone poplar tree near the Bridge of No Return at PanMunJom lay the bloodied remains of Arthur Bonifas and Mark Barrett. Captain Kim, four U.S. and four ROK soldiers were wounded.

"Although at the time of the melee, the cameras located at the UNC guard posts did not deter the incident, they recorded this brutal, unprovoked attack by the KPA guards," wrote Colonel DeLateur. "Soon the entire world would witness their immoral attack, in graphic detail, to the chagrin of North Korea."

THE AFTERMATH

Camp Greaves, headquarters for the 2/9th Infantry Battalion is located a few miles south of the DMZ. On August 18, 1976, when the alert siren blared, many soldiers at Greaves figured it was just another exercise to see how quickly they could respond to an all-out attack from North Korea. Still, they had to play the game to prove their combat readiness, so everyone quickly but without panic prepared to move out to their battle positions. Weapons and gas masks were drawn from the arms room and field gear was loaded onto rucksacks.

Most of the soldiers at Greaves were too busy getting their personal gear ready to even notice a military sedan from the JSA speed up to battalion headquarters. An Air Force captain jumped out and immediately called for volunteers to help transport a gravely injured man to a medical evacuation helicopter standing by.

Specialist 4 Carlton Tyler, a clerk typist with the 2/9th, was one of the first soldiers to see the badly wounded officer, Lt. Mark Barrett, and the extent of his injuries.

"There was blood everywhere. As soon as I saw him I felt sympathy for him and his family, because I knew his chances were slim. The more I thought about what happened, the angrier I got, and I felt a strong resentment, more than I've always felt, for the North Koreans just over the hill. Right then I knew this wasn't an average alert."

As the news of the incident spread like a wildfire, emotions ran at a fever-pitch among the soldiers stationed at Camp Greaves. Some were angry about the brutality of the unprovoked attack at PanMunJom. Many were scared, thinking of the unavoidable skirmish they were about to seek out just down the road. Most reacted from instinct as infantrymen. (Up until late 1978, the 2/9th Infantry Manchu Battalion was the first line of defense, the sacrificial lambs, if North Korea attacked the South).

What started out as just another alert became mayhem. Personal letters and photographs were destroyed—"Don't let the enemy find anything that could be used later to harass and terrorize relatives back home"—nonessential belongings were discarded, and everyone scribbled quick letters to their loved ones in case the worst happened.

Back at the JSA, where the incident occurred, the guards who were attacked explained the incident to others and soon the entire UN guard contingent was ready to strike back immediately, but the news hadn't even reached Eighth Army headquarters or the UNC in Seoul yet, so a quick counteroffensive would have to wait until approved.

Once word of the incident was transmitted to the 2nd Division Tactical Operations Center at Camp Casey, all units within the division were alerted. One such unit was the 1st Battalion of the 38th Field Artillery, which was wrapping up an Army Training Exercise, or ARTEP. Lieutenant Colonel Douglas Nickelson, recalled that late that afternoon on August 18, the 1st Battalion, 38th Field Artillery was in what was thought the last few days of an ARTEP at Nightmare Range. "However, word circulated to prepare to move and we did," Nickelson said. "Though we assumed we had not fared well on a move and we were being forced to Retest. Eventually we would march order back to Camp Stanley which had me wondering, was this a good thing or a bad thing? A glance around Headquarters and Headquarters Battery caused me to think we were a worn out, filthy bunch."

After completing the ARTEP, many of the soldiers in the battalion immediately took time off, and quickly left the battalion area before anyone knew what had happened in PanMunJom. "So left with the remainder of the battalion fire direction center vehicles and equipment, three others and myself began the cleanup tasks only to have that cut short a few hours later by the alert siren going off," recalled Nickelson. "It was at this point that a call for officers and NCOs spread. Fast forward, the meeting was simple: prepare for combat operations. It was then we received the first of a few briefings on what had occurred in the joint security area (JSA). We jumped from DEFCON 4 to DEFCON 3 in a matter of a few hours, with a prepare to assume DEFCON 2 on order."

For those soldiers who had taken leave, they eventually found out about the attack and attempted to rush back to their unit but the ROKs had shut down the main road from Seoul to the north.

Nickelson was then tasked "as a fire support liaison because the fire support section officer in charge knew me as a forward observer from our time with the 7th Field Artillery at Ft Riley, Ks. So off I go with a KATUSA and a U.S. soldier driver to find and establish fire support with the 38th Infantry."

ITCHING FOR PAYBACK

Soon night fell. Though annoyed that they didn't return to the tree site immediately, the UN guards still had a quiet confidence that an appropriate response would be forthcoming, "a kind of sixth sense that the United States would take some kind of action," stated Captain Ed Shirron, Joint Security Force commander at the time, who had the difficult task of restraining his men, some who'd been involved in the confrontation with Lt. Pak Chol and company at the tree site.

The entire 2nd Infantry Division was armed to the teeth and itching for a fight in just a few hours. Infantry, armor, aviation, and artillery units were prepped and loaded with a full array of ordnance for the expected move into the DMZ.

The following day an emergency session of the Washington Special Action Group—involving Secretary of State Henry Kissinger, CIA Chief George Bush, and Pentagon senior officers—was called to consider a variety of retaliatory options. After agreeing that the Tree Incident was premeditated, the group decided that a symbolic, rather than an "eye for an eye" response was necessary. The focal point of the killings, that sprawling poplar tree, would have to be cut down without question, but all forces in the area, would have to be prepared for a rapid escalation of the conflict.

Throughout Korea, military personnel were immediately called to full alert. All leaves were canceled and soldiers due to rotate back to the states were put on indefinite hold. Air Force jets and Army Honest John rockets were armed with both conventional and nuclear warheads aimed at enemy positions along the DMZ and industrial areas around the North Korean capital of Pyongyang.

After conferring with President Gerald Ford (in Kansas City for the Republican Convention), Kissinger briefed the WSAG on what was to transpire during the next few days in and around the Korean Peninsula.

CONVERGING ON THE NORTH PACIFIC

A Navy battle group led by the carrier Midway had already departed Yokosuka, Japan for Korean waters. Air Force fighter jets—24 Phantoms from Okinawa and twenty F-111s based at Mountain Home in Idaho—were scrambled and rushed to Korean airbases. B-52s from Guam would also head to the northwest Pacific and converge on PanMunJom as zero hour approached.

Closer to the anticipated killing ground "the whole atmosphere was very tense," stated PFC Donald Keith, a Redeye missile gunner from the Manchus at Camp Greaves. "All you could do was try to go quietly crazy during the endless wait."

Another soldier from the 2/9th, Staff Sergeant Raymond Garretson noted, "Morale went up one hundred percent the minute we knew this incident was more serious than the others. Everybody was ready to kick some ass, and mostly we were just plain mad at Joe Chink for what he'd done to those two officers."

DENYING THE CHARGES

The North Koreans, on the other hand, in the personage of the chief North Korean delegate at PanMunJom, General Han Ju Kyong, was claiming it was the Americans who had instigated the attack. And when U.S. Admiral Mark P. Frudden, senior member of the UN delegation, displayed detailed photographs of the incident, Han countered with his own evidence—an axe seized near the poplar tree still stained with the blood of a "North Korean soldier."

Despite the photos that clearly revealed as many as eight Communists wielding axes and metal tent pegs or pikes stabbing and beating one American, Han insisted the North Koreans had been forced "to defend themselves against this [American] aggression."

THE NEVER-ENDING WAIT

For two days the American soldiers in and around PanMunJom waited for word to strike. Some type of retaliatory action was imminent, but no one knew exactly what would happen, or when. Many combat veterans wanted to attack immediately after the incident occurred, before the enemy, also on full alert, could counter it . . . but still both sides waited.

They weren't sure who was going to make the final call or when. The 2nd Division commander? Eighth Army or UNC in Seoul? Maybe U.S. Pacific Command in Hawaii? After countless other incidents in the DMZ where many more Americans had been killed, it was highly unlikely a response to this incident would have to be made by the White House, but that is exactly where the debate was raging and where the decision to go in would be called.

The tension drove hard on everyone's mind, and for some American soldiers the strain began to show. Minor fights broke out, and a few soldiers even cried—they were afraid of dying, but no one wanted to be left out of the fight. As the second day grew longer with still no news from the decision makers, many soldiers along the DMZ thought the United States would back off, send everyone home, and just forget about the incident; a decision that would be "pure chicken-shit" stated one of the Manchus at Camp Greaves. But on the night of August 20 the order was finally given: "That damn tree will come down in the morning."

Earlier that day, Kimpo Airport was shut down for an hour while a solemn farewell ceremony was held for Captain Bonifus and Lieutenant Barrett as their caskets were loaded on a plane bound for the states.

In D.C., various options were still being considered. The proposal of dropping laser-guided "smart" bombs on the tree was scratched. Not wanting to display a warlike footing in the truce village, President Ford decided that no weapons would be used, no shots would be fired in cutting down the poplar tree, unless the North Koreans fired first. Only then would the presence of the fully armed Air Force planes and Navy battle group come into play, quickly and decisively.

Lieutenant Mike Kline, third platoon leader for Company A, 2/9th, selected to spearhead the mission, talked with his men during that sleepless night of August 20 once they knew the green light was on.

"All my people knew they were going into the Joint Security Area in the morning, and they all thought they weren't coming out. It was like we were going to be marching through the gates of Hell."

Kline had tried to calm his men as best he could, but some soldiers broke down and had to get away from the others, to release some of the pent-up tension.

"If we needed anything that night it was a chaplain," Kline recalled. "I did what I could to ease the tension, and explained that we weren't going in alone, that there would be all kinds of support for us, but I was as scared as they were."

The sleepless night of August 20 ended as the sun broke the horizon.

AUGUST 21, 1976

The Lord is my shepherd; I shall not want. He maketh me to lie down in green pastures: he leadeth me beside the still waters. He restoreth my soul: he leadeth me in the paths of righteousness for his name's sake. Yea, though I walk through the valley of the shadow of death, I will fear no evil: for thou art with me; thy rod and thy staff, they comfort me. Thou preparest a table before me in the presence of mine enemies: thou annointest my head with oil; my cup runneth over. Surely goodness and mercy shall follow me all the days of my life; and I will dwell in the house of the Lord forever.

Some of the Manchu soldiers changed the words slightly, a little black humor to a very serious situation: "Yea, though I walk through the valley of the shadow of death, I will fear no evil, for I am the meanest son of a bitch on the planet!"

"The valley of the shadow of death" is exactly where Operation Paul Bunyan would be carried out. Only three days before, at the same location, two American officers died in the shadow of that lone poplar tree. On the morning of August 21 another group of American and South Korean soldiers waited outside Camps Liberty Bell and Greaves to move into the JSA and "cut that damn tree down." The prayer was given, followed by orders to move out smartly.

ALPHA COMPANY SPEARHEADS THE MISSION

The entire 2/9th Infantry Battalion was involved in the mission, though only the third platoon from Company A actually entered the JSA. Company B and C were airborne, along with D Troop—the Delta Blues from the 4/7th Cavalry—all circling near the DMZ in twenty-six helicopter gunships while other elements of the 2/9th took up ground positions on both sides of the Imjin River. The stay-behinds at Greaves and Liberty Bell were busy rigging explosive charges to most of the buildings, while missile-loaded jeeps were aimed at the remaining structures.

One Redeye (missile) gunner remembered how he felt that morning while waiting for word to execute his part of the mission: "We never really knew how serious this was, I guess because there've been other incidents here where many more soldiers had been killed, and nothing was done in retaliation. But when they broke out the Redeyes all I could think was 'Oh God, here it comes.' That's when we knew, when everyone realized we were on the brink of war . . . all we could worry about was being wiped out if Joe Chink attacked."

Numerous contingencies were considered, in response to the brutal murder of two American Army officers at PanMunJom. With B-52 bombers flying overhead, Cobra gunships for close air support, and a Quick Reaction Force both in the air and on the ground, Operation Paul Bunyan kicked off a few days later, as North Korean guards watched it unfold. 2nd Division Museum photo.

ROK special forces troops—all of them black belt experts in Tae Kwon Do and armed with clubs—took up position to block any North Korean advance from Guard Post #5.

Farther south the 2/17th Field Artillery had its guns pointed at strategic targets along the western sector of the DMZ, while Air Force fighter jets prowled overhead, and the B-52s conducted mock bombing runs along the southern edge of the DMZ, ever-ready on a moment's notice to open their bomb bay doors, veer north, and drop their ordnance. All of these planes, primed for battle, were prepared to devastate the Communist capital of Pyongyang if anything happened at PanMunJom, "in the valley of the shadow of death."

DIVISION COMMANDER PROUD OF HIS TROOPS

Major General Morris J. Brady, who had assumed command of the 2nd Infantry Division less than two months prior, explained the timetable of Operation

Paul Bunyan as it happened on that morning, and remembered his feelings as he watched the mission from his command helicopter.

"We rolled at 0648 and hit the line of departure at 0700 on the nose. It was a proud moment for this Division because we had it all together—the training, the maintenance and the discipline—to get the job done.

"The task force moved into the JSA right on schedule. Everything was orderly and unhurried. There were some illegal road barriers there so we pulled them right out of the ground. The North Koreans were caught completely by surprise—they were bewildered and confused. Although they were armed, they made no move to challenge us. As they watched, we turned the tree into kindling wood. By 0800 it was over and we left as we had come—on time, in order and full of pride." (As the operation unfolded, the 150 North Korean soldiers, armed with side arms and AK-47s, arrived on the west side of the Bridge of No Return, but took no provocative action, probably calculating that the numbers didn't favor them.)

(Several eye-witnesses on board General Brady's helicopter have confirmed that it was fired on by a North Korean soldier and was forced to land during Operation Paul Bunyan.)

"Of great concern to the leadership at all levels was the possible intervention by the KPA (Korean People's Army), which could have resulted in bloodshed," wrote Colonel DeLateur. "The reasons for nonintervention by the KPA during the operation are not readily discernable, but were probably a combination of military and political factors. The speed and surprise achieved by the UNC forces caught the KPA unprepared, and possibly unwilling, to react with violence. Once inside the JSA, the determined, professional actions of the ROK and U.S. soldiers may have intimidated the KPA soldiers and made them reluctant to respond actively. The North Korean Government was embarrassed internationally by this incident, and therefore hesitant to compound their loss of face through another incident, especially one for which they were not completely prepared."

A few weeks after the successful PanMunJom mission, Brady expressed his thoughts to the entire 2nd Infantry Division: "As we proved to ourselves we could do it, we proved to a watching world. America is a compassionate and forgiving country. Some may take that as a sign of weakness. It isn't. It is a sign of strength that shows itself when America is pushed too far. We will not allow others to force us to give up rights of free movement in the JSA guaranteed to us in the Armistice Agreement. That is why we cut down the tree.

"I have talked to you before about the spirit of this Division. I told you then it was our greatest asset. On that Saturday morning, when we moved out to do the job that had been given us, I saw that spirit in action and I was tremendously proud—proud of you for your resolute professionalism, proud of this powerful Division and proud to be an American soldier."

That pride wasn't just reserved for the 2nd Division commander.

Lieutenant Mike Kline, the third platoon leader who'd wished there had been a chaplain with his men the night before they entered the JSA, added, "The whole time they were cutting the tree, a great feeling of pride filled me. I think it was in all of us. We were proud to be there, proud to be Americans, and something I hadn't experienced before—an immense pride in wearing the U.S. Army uniform."

As the tree hit the ground, U.S. and ROK Army soldiers joined together, cheering loudly while nearby North Korean soldiers were dumbfounded, afraid to move either forward or back. It was a proud moment for everyone there, but it could just as easily have been a killing ground, as it already had been three days before.

"One bullet could have started a total war," explained 2/9th Infantry Battalion commander Lieutenant Colonel Ken Hightower. "We had a very pressure-packed situation, and every man had live ammo. It's to the credit of the men in my command that they had the maturity and foresight to handle the situation without firing a single shot."

If the North Korean soldier that fired on General Brady's helicopter that day had succeeded in shooting it down or wounded someone on board, or had lowered his sites and killed an American soldier on the ground, that would have been "one bullet that started a total war," which was on the minds of every one of the million-odd troops deployed on both sides of the Demilitarized Zone, prowling the waters off Korea, and flying overhead. The potential for World War III was but one bullet removed.

The August 18, 1976, Tree Incident is now just a vague memory to most Americans. Even soldiers newly deployed to South Korea know little about "what happened in the DMZ more than three decades ago."

But *Korea Herald* reporter Lee, Won Sul explained, "Inundated by the propaganda that all Americans are 'imperialists' bent on conquering the whole world, North Korean soldiers—particularly those who are hand-picked by the Communist Party for their unswerving loyalty to serve in PanMunJom—seem to have a genuine hatred toward their American counterparts. With their hatred aglow, these robotized men have become totally inflexible in their thoughts. Viewed in this sense, the PanMunJom incident is not going to be the last one. The same can be repeated at any place, at any time, on any condition."

> The danger of the past was that men became slaves. The danger of the future is that men may become robots. —Erich Fromm

PROPHESY COME TRUE

He wrote constantly about the dangers of Korea's Demilitarized Zone, saying "You never know . . . anything can happen." But to assure loved ones at home, the young American soldier always ended his letters with, "I can take care of myself." Two weeks before he was due to return home though, the man was dead, butchered when North Korean soldiers beat him with axes and pikes. He left a wife and three children behind to bury him and to accept a letter of condolence. Yet nothing was done in retaliation . . . except chop down a poplar tree, which seems like a meek response.

DRAMATIC CHANGE IN THE JSA

"As the tensions began to wane, the UNC's Rear Admiral Frudden opened the 380th MAC meeting by calling for punishment of those responsible for the murders and insisting on assurances for the future safety and freedom of activity of the UNC personnel," wrote Colonel DeLateur. "Citing the presence of armed personnel of the two sides in a limited area, Major General Han, the KPA's senior member, proposed each side be restricted to their respective sides of the Military Demarcation Line (MDL) within the JSA. On 6 September, the Senior Members approved the changes to the Military Armistice Agreement that included: jointly establish and mark the MDL through the JSA (first time since 1953), restrict military members from crossing the MDL into the opposing side, require each side to insure the safety of all who legally transit the MDL, and prohibit construction of barriers that obstruct observation of the opposing side."

JOURNAL

I arrived in country one year after the Tree Incident and it was a little tense. A lot of guys were edgy, as rumors spread that the North Koreans might cause a little mischief to remember that "heroic" day. We tend to consider it more of an act of cowardice on their part.

(Coincidentally, a year ago when the incident occurred, President Ford was in Kansas City for his party's convention and I shot some photos of him while I was home in leave. Halfway around the world, the men of the 2nd Infantry Division were preparing for war, but back home, while deciding their fate, President Ford had some campaigning to do. His opponent was Jimmy Carter, who vowed to remove U.S. troops from South Korea.)

• 5 •

Shangri-la

Inside the World's Deadliest Border

Never pretend to be a unicorn by sticking a plunger on your head. —Martín Espada, 2006

*A*n amazing and unbelievable phenomenon has occurred between the Southern and Northern Barrier fences of the DMZ over these many years of perilous truce. With the freedom to roam across the MDL without prompting a violation of the Armistice Agreement, thousands of rare endangered animals and birds thrive. With the exception of two villages in the eastern sector of the zone—one in the south, one in the north, both near PanMunJom—the heavily fortified swath across the Korean Peninsula is a protected sanctuary for wildlife and plant life, especially in the central and eastern sectors, which are mountainous and largely inaccessible.

Among the rare, precious, and few are the Amur leopard, Korean tiger, and Asian black bear, the red-crowned crane, and white-naped crane. Biologists and ecologists perched along the Southern Barrier Fence with long lens scopes have documented seventy types of mammals, more than three hundred species of birds, and nearly three thousand varieties of plants.

In his insightful book *The Impossible State*, Victor Cha wrote: "Once you enter [the DMZ], it is like an oasis. The vista turns beautifully green as you enter land that has literally been untouched and undisturbed by human hands for sixty years. Nature has thrived in this space out of the destruction of war beyond anyone's imagination. It is literally a piece of Eden in the middle of a military standoff. The area is adorned by natural waterfalls, and tourists today can hike areas adjacent to the DMZ leading to Daeam Mountain. A typical and unforgettable sight was empty shell casings and a rotted-out army helmet sitting amid a field of bright yellow wildflowers, literally untouched for over half a century because the area remains a live minefield."

During a visit to South Korea, journalist Ian Buruma took the obligatory bus tour to PanMunJom and noted, in the October 2003 issue of *Travel and Leisure* magazine: "When we had finally passed through several checkpoints and entered the Dora Observatory, where a South Korean soldier waited to

The Korean Demilitarized Zone is a wildlife paradise for thousands of rare and endangered animals, including two species of cranes. Photo by Gary L. Bloomfield.

point out to us the landmarks of the DMZ, we were confronted with the most astonishing view. For there in front of us was a vision of paradise, a vast tract of dense forest, a river and misty hills, straight out of a traditional Korean painting. You could just make out the gigantic flag of North Korea's Propaganda Village, facing the equally absurd flag of South Korea's Freedom Village. These were the only signs of human habitation. Fifty years of heavily armed truce had turned this old battlefield into a nature reserve, inhabited by Siberian cranes, Mongolian eagles, and many rare species of flora and fauna. It was one of the most beautiful places I had seen in Korea."

Though not spotted in the vicinity of the DMZ, traces of another mythical beast have been uncovered near Pyongyang. Such a magnificent creature had not been seen in centuries and many even wondered if it had ever existed. In recent years though, archeologists have found and have verified the lair of a unicorn, and not just any run-of-the-mill unicorn. This one was ridden by the founder of the Koguryo Kingdom—Tongmyong—sometime between 2,000 and 2,200 years ago. This amazing discovery proves that the true birthplace of the Koguryo Kingdom is in the north. Of course no one dare challenge this historic find . . . at least no one north of the DMZ dares to question it.

Though not "endangered," there is one small plot of terra firma inside the DMZ that is considered the world's most dangerous of its kind, located at Camp Bonifas at PanMunJom. It is two football fields long, give or take a few feet, with barbed wire and minefields just feet away, yet close enough to cause problems for those who venture to navigate its bunkers and hazards.

Located at Camp Bonifas near PanMumJom is the world's most dangerous golf course. The par 3, one hole "course" is bordered by minefields and barbed-wire fencing, with North Korea just beyond its out of bounds marker. Photo by *Soldier* magazine.

Reporting for the 8th Army Public Affairs Office, Walter T. Ham IV wrote in September 2009, "The most dangerous golf course in the world is one here where an extra-long drive can land your ball in a minefield, a slice can lob it into a hillside Army bunker and a hook can deposit it in a ginseng field."

For those golfers with less-than-deadly accuracy, it is strongly advised that if a tee shot does go astray, and bounces off the course, just to let it lie, and that's of course if it didn't set off any of the mines littered beyond the fairway and the green.

· 6 ·

Agent Orange

A Deadly Legacy

Author's Note: When I was managing editor for *VFW* magazine, I wrote an article about the spraying of Agent Orange in Vietnam. I had heard rumors about its use along the Korean DMZ when I was stationed there, but at the time no one considered the long-term health issues for those exposed to it. While the following is about Vietnam, there are several parallels to Korea— primarily why Agent Orange was used, the health problems that developed years later, and the fight to prove that exposure.

AGENT ORANGE SPRAYING IN VIETNAM AND, AT THE SAME TIME, THE KOREAN DMZ

The Spring of 1969, Ca Mau Peninsula, South Vietnam . . . Navy patrol boats have begun probing the tributaries of the Mekong River in an effort to cut off enemy supply routes from Cambodia. Dense jungle foliage, however, conceals Viet Cong (VC) guerillas waiting all along the waterways to ambush the vulnerable American intruders.

Though sampans loaded with enemy arms and supplies are being stopped and destroyed, U.S. losses continue to mount. The VC lash out with deadly effectiveness, concentrating a barrage of automatic weapons fire, mortars, and floating mines on the highly armored American patrol boats that wander into undetected traps along the narrow streams and rivers.

Despite the escalating casualty count, Navy patrol boats must continue, day and night, in an attempt to stop the weapons flow, because American ground forces are taking a pounding from the almost-invisible but heavily armed VC.

Admiral Elmo Zumwalt Jr., commander of the inland Navy patrol boats (nicknamed the "Brown Water Navy") is faced with the dilemma of how to continue the vital search and destroy missions yet somehow reduce American losses, which are excessively high and personally intolerable. With his own son commanding one of the patrol boats, Admiral Zumwalt knows the odds are against his namesake and crew.

"Our river patrol casualties reached an unacceptably high rate," noted Admiral Zumwalt in his book *My Father, My Son.*

Chemical defoliants, intended to turn the lush jungles into barren wasteland where the VC could no longer hide, seem to be the only "quick-fix" solution. After assurances from the Army, the Air Force, and the manufacturers that there are no serious or long-lasting side-effects, Admiral Zumwalt orders the spraying of Agent Orange along every river and tributary patrolled by the Navy.

"I had strong feelings for the young men who were out in the field, fighting the war, risking and sometimes losing their lives. No commander who cares about his men can escape those feelings," recalled the admiral. "I based my decision to use Agent Orange on my desire to minimize casualties. As more and more Agent Orange was sprayed, our patrol boat casualties begin to drop significantly, so our strategy was obviously succeeding."

It was neither an easy nor a callous decision. Agent Orange was a necessity of war, an effective weapon used to neutralize the enemy and in turn, improve the odds of survival for the Brown Water Navy's warriors. (At the same time, barrels of Agent Orange were being sent to South Korea, Guam, and other American outposts, including some stateside locations.)

"Drastic changes took place before our eyes," recalled Elmo Zumwalt III, commander of one of the Navy patrol boats, and son of the admiral. "One week there would be thick green foliage, and the next we would see leaves and grass eaten away from the devastating effects of Agent Orange. I felt safe knowing that if [the Viet Cong] wanted to ambush us, at least they would no longer shoot us from point-blank range" as they had done before the defoliation.

Though care was taken to ensure that chemical spraying was not done while Navy patrol boats were actually in the vicinity, it was virtually impossible for the crews to avoid coming in contact with the chemical contaminants.

"I had often walked around in these defoliated areas and washed and waded in the rivers and canals into which Agent Orange had drained," Lt. Zumwalt wrote several years later.

"We ate fruits and vegetables we bought from the local Vietnamese, which I suspected were doused with Agent Orange. I remember having a skin rash I thought might have been caused by the sun, but I have since learned that one of the effects of Agent Orange exposure is a skin rash. But at the time, I was thankful for the defoliation." (American troops in Korea, tramping through rice paddies, and wading in the Imjin River, were also exposed to contaminated waters polluted with Agent Orange.)

In the Spring of 1979, Admiral Zumwalt was selected to become chief of naval operations in Washington, D.C. His son would be following him "back to the world" a few months later.

"After more than nine months as a swift boat officer, after firefights and ambushes too numerous to count, after being scared, sick, exhausted, angry, frustrated, saddened, and challenged in ways I never imagined before, I found I could cope with everything," remembered Lt. Zumwalt.

"When I finally boarded the plane at Ton Son Nhut Airport to leave Vietnam, I had an indescribable feeling of exhilaration and relief knowing I was really getting out . . . I had been very lucky in Vietnam."

Little did he know that his life and death struggle to survive in Vietnam would follow him back to the states, and in a few years another enemy—just as relentless, and even more elusive than the Viet Cong—would challenge him again.

Marines from the 5th Marine Regiment patrol southwest of Danang, South Vietnam, in waters contaminated by Agent Orange. GIs in Korea patrolled along the Imjin River near the DMZ, unaware that it too had been sprayed and contaminated with the defoliant. Marine Corps photo.

Though Vietnam remained a haunting nightmare, Elmo Zumwalt was ready to pick up the pieces and return to the normalcy of civilian life. "The fear, the horrendous living conditions, and all the killing were not experiences I ever wanted to repeat. I was more certain than ever that I did not want to make the Navy my career. I wanted out."

Within a few months of returning from Vietnam, he resigned his commission, married a long-time sweetheart, and became a college student again, enrolling in law school. "I still carried scars from my Vietnam experiences, but the psychological problems I experienced as a returning veteran were small because I belong to a supportive family that had a very clear understanding of what I had been through."

The idyllic family setting seemed complete when, in 1977, Elmo and Kathy Zumwalt became the proud parents of Elmo R. Zumwalt IV, nicknamed Russell, "a beautiful, healthy-looking baby," Elmo boasted. "But within two or three months Kathy became suspicious that something was wrong. Russell was slower in his early phases of development. He was slow to lift his head, crawl, sit up and walk."

Their concern heightened when Russell began nursery school and his teacher noticed his learning difficulties. "At about this time, Kathy and I became aware through press and television accounts that many Vietnam veterans whose children had been born with serious defects believed their exposure to Agent Orange might be responsible."

Compounding the emotional trauma of his son's disability was the news that Elmo was also suffering from multiple ailments, diagnosed as cancer.

"The thought that Agent Orange might be connected with my cancer more than crossed my mind, especially in light of Russell's learning problems," he realized. "Recent reports from Vietnamese medical authorities reported high rates of birth defects and illness in areas where Agent Orange had been heavily sprayed.

"At first I had dismissed these reports as propaganda, but with our own Vietnam veterans now claiming a link, coupled with experience in my own family, they looked more plausible to me."

Once again, just as he had done in Vietnam, Elmo Zumwalt was fighting an unseen enemy that was just as intent on destroying him as the Viet Cong had been, only this time his own son had become an innocent victim.

It would be a long, drawn-out battle, much like Vietnam, with minor victories, major setbacks, and little hope of defeating this unsympathetic killer known as Agent Orange. But he was determined to fight this battle to the end, hoping for a cure, yet admitting that his chances were slim.

"I guess we all wonder how we will react when we realize our time is short," wrote Elmo during one of his many setbacks. "For me, there is value in having a terminal illness rather than dying suddenly. It has allowed me to prepare for my family's future, and it focused my mind on the important things in life, such as spending time with the people I love.

"I feel the worst thing I could do would be to dwell on thoughts of death and be miserable every day. I have tried to mentally shut out depressing thoughts and live every day as valuably as I could."

Though physically unharmed, the one man who suffers the most mental anguish is Elmo's father, Russell's grandfather . . . Admiral Zumwalt.

"Because of the orders I gave to step up defoliation in the Ca Mau Peninsula there is no question in my mind that, indirectly at least, I was responsible for Elmo's heavy exposure to Agent Orange, which makes me an instrument in his tragedy. What has happened to Russell and Elmo deepens my own

Author's Note: In early 1990 I flew to Washington, D.C., to meet with Admiral Zumwalt for this story, published in *VFW* magazine in April of that year. The admiral was still mourning the death of his son just two years earlier. And his grandson was also dealing with birth defects attributable to his dad's exposure to Agent Orange. Whenever I visit D.C. I always stop by the Vietnam Memorial Wall in memory of my father, Army Command Sergeant Major Robert D. Bloomfield, who had the difficult task of escorting the remains of senior noncommissioned officers (NCOs) from Vietnam to their home, for burial with full military honors.

After my meeting with Admiral Zumwalt I asked if he would go with me to the Wall, but he politely declined, saying it was still too painful to see the names on the Wall, the names of His Boys of the Brown Water Navy.

In January 2000, Admiral Elmo Zumwalt passed away. First and foremost he is known as one of our nation's commanders of the Vietnam War. But he was also a proud father and loving grandfather. As I concluded the article for *VFW* magazine twelve years before his death, I wanted readers to know that side of him. The memory of a loving son, the struggle to help raise a gifted grandson, and the frequent contact with disabled veterans are constant reminders of Admiral Zumwalt's personal and tragic legacy. He endured that personal tragedy with a heavy heart, when he stated: "It is the first thing I think of when I awake in the morning, and the last thing I remember when I go to sleep at night."

For veterans stationed along the Korean DMZ, they too were exposed to the spraying of Agent Orange, used to decimate dense foliage around outposts and guard posts and compounds, and along patrol routes, in an effort to eliminate enemy ambush sites. And, just as Vietnam veterans fight to prove debilitating health problems are attributable to their exposure to Agent Orange, DMZ vets are doing likewise, searching for witnesses and documentation to verify their claims for VA compensation and medical care.

sense of futility about the Vietnam War. I regard Elmo and Russell as casualties of that war. I realized that had I not used Agent Orange, many more lives would have been lost in combat, perhaps even Elmo's. But that does not ease the sorrow I feel for Elmo, or the anguish his illness, and Russell's disability, gives me."

In 1988, Elmo Zumwalt lost his fight against the aftereffects of Agent Orange. Never, even during the worst periods of his illness, did he vent any hostilities toward his father for ordering the spraying of Agent Orange in Vietnam.

"I do not second-guess the decisions Dad made, nor do I doubt that the saving of human life was always his first priority in his conduct of the war. I have the greatest love and admiration for him as a man, and the deepest respect for him as a military leader.

"Certainly thousands are alive today because of his decision to use Agent Orange. I do not hold him responsible for what has happened to Russell and me."

AN IMJIN SCOUT STRUGGLES WITH
AGENT ORANGE EXPOSURE

Army Sergeant Dennis Urban served on the Korean DMZ in 1968 and 1969—

" . . . in late July '68 I was assigned to Company B, 1st Battalion, 9th Infantry, 2nd Infantry Division. Two short days at South Camp Custer and Captain Sawyer shipped my ass to the fence and Zone for training. So as the guys got ready to pack it up and leave, I got to gain all of their infinite wisdom for two full weeks . . . day and night . . . didn't see the sack the whole time I think, but I got a tour of the Zone.

"Agent Orange was unknown to the troops in Korea. The government didn't admit the fact that it was used until after 1980. We all knew that something had been sprayed on the guard posts in the DMZ, all along the barrier fence as well as out into the fifty-yard wide minefield and the ten-yard safe zone. In the camps north of the river you seldom saw any grass or anything else growing.

"There was more than Agent Orange used. There was a 'rainbow' of agents. Orange was just one of them. They also used Agent Green for pine trees and similar trees and bushes, Agent White, and I believe Agent Blue. American troops and vehicles were used to mix the chemicals in five-ton trucks with fuel tanks, pumps, and hoses. After daybreak they would cross the bridges (either Freedom Bridge or Libby Bridge) and add the chemicals into the diesel fuel tanks on the back of the five-ton truck. My understanding is it was a 10 percent chemical to 90 percent diesel fuel mix. Now, once it was mixed, the truck or trucks would proceed to whatever area they were assigned to spray that day.

"If the wind was blowing north, they would spray along the barrier fence itself, arcing the spray high into the air so that the wind would carry it out as far as possible into the Z. You have to understand, when the barrier fence was put up, it did NOT follow the Southern Demarcation Line. It sometimes was south of the line, sometimes north of the line, sometimes on the line. It was placed where we had the best chance for a line of site view, for a possible infiltrator coming thru the lines. The spray thus followed that fence line for over twelve and a half miles of the American lines.

"Where they couldn't spray from the trucks, they used backpack hand pumps. Now comes the interesting part, which I verified at the 100th Anniversary Convention of the 2nd Infantry Division. When the crew was done for the day, they were not allowed to cross the bridges with any of the mixture. So, to 'safely' get rid of it, they would open a spray bar across the back of the truck as they drove down the numerous dirt roads that were north of the river. They really thought that by doing this, they were knocking down the dust on the roads. The roads quickly absorbed the liquids, and dried out in little time. Now, when the next group of trucks came down those same roads loaded with troops, the dust went airborne and was sucked into the lungs and coated the faces and hands of the soldiers.

"The Agent Orange and the diesel fuel was breathed in for ten, fifteen, maybe twenty minutes or more on every trip, both ways. The troops went on those roads every day, sometimes twice a day, depending on their assignments. Then, once the tanks were empty, they went to a place on the Imjin River bank where the engineers had cut away a place to drive down into the river a few feet. At this point, water was drawn into the tanks, slushed around, and all the piping and hoses were flushed out into the river. Gallons of mix every day would go into the river, the same river that the Korean civilians fished, bathed, and drew drinking water and cooking water from!!!

"Other ways we were exposed was patrolling thru bushes and weeds that had been sprayed. It got into our drinking water supplies, the contaminated dust was everywhere. You just could not get away from it. Even camps south of the river had their perimeter fences sprayed. Everyone could see that the grass and weeds around their positions . . . be it on the guard posts or on the fence areas . . . was brown in color and dead, in the middle of summer when everywhere else it was green and growing.

"It was a good seventy-five yards from the outside of the minefield to the back of the trench/foxhole positions, and everything was brown. The distance between positions varied by terrain . . . if it was really hilly country, they were closer. If it was flat country, they were further apart.

I'd guess the average position was close to one hundred yards from the next one on either side.

"You have to understand that General Charles Bonesteel of 8th Army Command came up with the DMZ fence and positions plan. It was his baby. Before 1968 there was no barrier fence, just a series of trenches and foxholes scattered along an imaginary line on the ground. There was a Military Demarcation Line, and a Southern Line, but no actual 'fences' to see. At the MDL there was a single strand of barbed wire with worn out pieces of white engineer tape. Some places the wire was totally gone. I believe the North Koreans would do this to trick us into crossing the MDL, which would be an armistice violation! Other places the wire was on the ground and grown over by the weeds."

Hundreds of Korea veterans—and not just those stationed along the DMZ—are fighting for VA compensation and medical care due to their exposure to Agent Orange. While it was well known that Agent Orange was used in Southeast Asia, for years it was denied in Korea (also in other overseas locations and even some stateside posts).

"[Department of Defense] has confirmed that Agent Orange was used from April 1968 up through July 1969 along the DMZ," states a Government Printing Office Fact Sheet—"Agent Orange/Herbicides used Outside of Vietnam," dated July 1, 2001. "DoD defoliated the fields of fire between the frontline defensive positions and the south barrier fence. The size of the treated area was a strip of lane 151 miles long and up to 350 yards wide from the fence to north of the 'civilian control line.' There is no indication that herbicide was sprayed in the DMZ itself.

"The estimated number of exposed personnel is 12,056."

Board of Veterans Appeal Citation #9906724, dated March 12, 1999, stated, "Official records confirm that herbicide agents were sprayed in South Korea from the Civilian Control Line to the southern boundary of the DMZ during 1968 and 1969. An official letter from the Department of the Army to Senator John Glenn, dated May 1996, reflects that official records show use of 21,000 gallons of Agent Orange in Korea in 1968 and 1969 in the area of the DMZ. This letter also states that Camp Casey was located in the area of the DMZ."

One veteran who was personally involved with spraying in Korea wrote, in June 2004:

"I, Steve Witter, served with the 2nd Inf. Division, Chemical Company. We were based out of Camp Howze, Korea from 1968–1969. The Chemical Company was responsible for the application of herbicides in the North, South, East and Western areas of Korea. Including areas in and around the

Soldiers from the 2nd of the 9th Infantry—the Manchus—patrol the Southern Barrier Fence of the DMZ. Agent Orange was sprayed extensively to cut down on places where North Korean infiltrators could wait to ambush the patrols. Photo by Gary L. Bloomfield.

Libby Bridge and Spoonbill Bridge which I believed was a pontoon bridge. We also traveled in and or near the DMZ. We also treated areas along and or near to the Imjin River with herbicide agents. We commonly traveled by means of these bridges. One bridge was also known as the Freedom Bridge. We also traveled from one camp to another.

"Upon our arrival at each camp we were required to document the locations we had completed spray missions. At this time we received instructions/orders as to other areas in need of attention. An escort from the camp would direct us to the location needing attention. High risk areas such as the DMZ required a Piper Cub plane to confirm the area was clear and safe in order that we could enter the location. Our missions occurred on a daily basis consisting of many areas which were treated with herbicide agents to include more than just areas along the DMZ.

"It was not uncommon for the chemical companies to spray locations throughout not only southern areas of Korea but also the Northern I Corps, including camp perimeters, mess hall areas, look out towers and some camp churches such as at Camp Howze. One of the lookout towers was located in an extremely steep area. Others on my truck would not ride up the incline in the truck due to the high elevation and dangers regarding the trip up the mountain.

"I found it odd the hoses and tires on the truck would soften like gum when exposed to the agents. The hoses on the tanks constantly melted causing them to break and created direct exposure. The rubber on the soles of our shoes would also turn soft and glue-like. At no time were we ever supplied protective equipment. We were never warned that the agents were hazardous nor told that we could not dump the chemicals on roadways, in rivers, and/or creek beds. We were never warned of the hazards of spray drift [wind].

"I understand that the herbicide agents were transported to Korea from Vietnam. They were flown into Kimpo [airport], Seoul, Korea. The agents would then be trucked into Camp Howze to a staging area. We would receive about thirty 55-gallon drums on a flatbed truck. The barrels were identified by a painted strip indicating the specific formula in the drum. Some of the herbicide agents were in powder form. All agents were combined with diesel in preparation for application. The agents were mixed in tanks on the decontamination trucks. The trucks were deuce and a halfs, with a 400 or 450 gallon tank attached to them. I was responsible for the maintenance of my truck, the tank and the mixing of the agents and on many occasions the application of the agents. Many times we found broken glass in the tanks as though it had been put there on purpose.

"On a daily basis, units out of Seoul [would] transport the agents [to] a staging area on the DMZ, or at a camp. This allowed us to address several locations in that particular area. The staging area also provided a safe location where we could fill our tanks in preparation for the duty missions and to perform any mechanical repairs. We usually filled the tanks twice a day. In some cases a three-quarter-ton truck with a trailer loaded with additional herbicide agents would accompany us to avoid us from having to return to the staging area. There were three or four trucks in my unit making these daily applications.

"Typically, after the applications of herbicide agents we found our skin and eyes would feel irritated, burning, leaving a grayish color to our skin. Within two days of treating a location we would return to the area and then burn it with napalm. My partner drove the truck of napalm. After burning the area, CS would then be applied by aerial methods which causes one to defecate, vomit and also feel burning of the eyes and skin.

"Because there weren't provisions in camps or at staging locations to dump the herbicide agents at day's end, we would open the valve to drain the tanks. It was common maintenance practice for us to release the remaining agents onto roadways, roadsides, on rivers including the Imjin River or into creek beds. We would release anywhere from 25 to 100 gallons of the agent before returning to camp to refill the tanks in preparation from the next day's duties. We would try to clean the trucks daily but due to some of our locations this would not always occur, causing others at staging areas to be exposed to the residual agent on the truck."

EXCERPTS FROM KEY AGENT ORANGE DOCUMENTS

Thousands of veterans who've served in Korea—and not just in the vicinity of the DMZ—may have been exposed to the spraying of Agent Orange and other defoliants along the DMZ and around military compounds and roadways. Veterans filing claims with the Department of Veterans Affairs face an uphill fight to prove exposure and its correlation to cancers and other ailments they're suffering from due to that exposure.

Following are excerpts from key classified or confidential documents that have been declassified in recent years:

- Toxic Defoliant Use in South Korea, dated 8 January 1980, to the Under Secretary of Defense for Research and Engineering: The South Korean "Defense Ministry admitted that Agent Orange and two other toxic defoliants, supplied by the U.S. forces, were sprayed along the DMZ in 1968 and 1969." "The South Korean Defense Ministry and the Pentagon verified a report that the U.S. Forces Korea first suggested the use of the defoliants in 1967. It supplied Agent Orange, Agent Blue and Monuron to South Korean Army soldiers, who were mobilized for the spraying mission. More than 59,000 gallons of the defoliants, including 21,000 gallons of the highly toxic Agent Orange, were spread on 20,794 acres of land along a 100-meter strip south of the 155-mile-long DMZ. Neither the South Korean nor the U.S. forces knew how toxic the defoliants were, and no proper warning was given to the soldiers involved in the spray mission." (Excerpt from the *Korea Herald* newspaper, December 6, 1999, which was included in the document.)
- Summary 1968 Vegetation Control Tests, Army Advisory Group, Korea, declassified December 30, 1975: "Defoliation operations have been conducted in Vietnam and Korea to improve visibility, thereby reducing the number of likely ambush sites from which an aggressor could inflict damage and/or casualties upon friendly personnel." "Chemicals were sent from the Plant Sciences Lab, Fort Detrick, to the Republic of Korea for the purpose of testing their effectiveness in the control of vegetation." "The use of chemical herbicides may cause

imagined damage to crops and aquatic wildlife outside the boundary of the barrier. Real damage may result due to drifting spray or surface run-off." "The defoliants Orange, Blue and Monuron were to provide a one-time treatment of 18,830 acres, equivalent to a strip 151 miles long by 342 yards wide. Application of Munuron began on 17 April on strips 200 meters in width along selected portions on the DMZ Security System Fence. On 25 April, the application of Monuron was completed in the I Corps area. A total of 145,000 pounds of Monuron (2,900 drums) was spread by hand for a total coverage area of 580 acres in the I Corps area."

- Herbicide Status Report, issued by the U.S. Army and Joint Services Environmental Support Group: "The name Agent Orange comes from the identifying orange stripe painted on drums containing a particular herbicide which contained equal proportions of . . . herbicides 2, 4-D and 2,4,5-T. Only 2,4,5-T has been implicated as causing any potential health problems, due to the presence of the toxic contaminant dioxin."

- Final Report, Vegetation Control Plan CY 68 (calendar year 1968), Army Advisory Group, Korea, January 2, 1969: "In 1963, CG I Corps proposed the use of herbicides in the DMZ to improve observation and fields of fire and to deny hostile forces the concealment provided by vegetation." "In early 1967, UNC/USFK found that cover, provided North Korean infiltration or raiding parties by the vegetation within the DMZ and contiguous areas, had grown unencumbered since the Armistice and was an important part of the DMZ defensive problem. Dense uncontrolled growth significantly hampers UNC defensive operations while enemy infiltration operations are enhanced. Effective use of night vision devices was affected by dense foliage and frequently movements of UN Forces into defensive positions were being hampered." "Defoliant applications were initiated on 15 April, 1968 with the application of Monuron. No particular difficulties were found in dispensing Monuron as it is spread by hand similar to the manner by which Korean farmers spread seeds or fertilizer . . . each man walked along his assigned lane spreading Monuron by hand or the mechanical spreader along approximately five meters on each side of his marked lane." "There were no problems encountered in the handling, storage or application of defoliant materials. It had been anticipated that some of the defoliants could possibly cause eye, nose, throat, and skin irritation; however, this effect was minimized by the wearing of gauze masks and gloves when handling the material and by washing upon completion of application." "Defoliant application teams employed deceptive measures in those areas under observation from North Korean outposts by labeling equipment and supplies with the code words 'CORN' for Monuron, 'RICE' for Agent Blue, and 'BEANS' for Agent Orange to give the impression that the working teams were planting crops."

• Annex E: Technical Characteristics of Herbicides: "the following defoliants were selected for use in Korea: Agent Orange is relatively non-toxic and no danger exists to warm blooded animals in connection with its handling and application. Agent Blue. Rice and other cereal grain crops . . . are extremely sensitive to this agent. In fact Blue has been used in Vietnam as a specific agent to destroy Viet Cong rice crops. Monuron OROX 22. It is comparatively non-toxic and no danger exists to man or animals in handling and application."

JOURNAL

Every morning at Camp Casey we had PT, followed by a two-mile run, sometimes around the bend to Camp Hovey. There was a shallow stream along the way and sometimes I would look over and see a rainbow color of oil and lubricant puddles, and whatever else was dumped in that stream, including possible herbicides, pesticides, and whatever other "cides" were used.

Whenever I went to the DMZ, I always carried at least two cameras—one for black and whites, one for color. Along the Southern Barrier Fence there was a wide strip of dirt, a string of sandbags, then a strip of dead and brown grasses and bushes, then lush greenery. Never thunk much of it, but now I realize the brown waste land had been sprayed with Agent Orange and other deadly concoctions.

Often I traveled back and forth to the DMZ via Huey helicopter and shot aerials whenever the side door was open. From the air, it was quite obvious where defoliants had been used. (It is possible burning or mowing was done to cut back the high grasses and brush around U.S. compounds along the Southern Barrier Fence and the road leading into the DMZ.) Curiously though, I typically took my color slides to the PX for processing and one time an entire roll of aerials I had shot at the DMZ were missing. The clerk at the photo booth said someone had confiscated the slides. At the time I just assumed I had possibly shot something classified, but now, many years later, I have to wonder if those slides revealed the extent of defoliation spraying, and someone didn't want those photos to someday be used as evidence. After that incident, I took my unprocessed film to the craft shop photo lab at Camp Casey and processed them myself.

· 7 ·

Cause of Death Unknown

So that's the end of GI Joe. And all the people at home hear that Joe is gone and they are sorry it happened and they add, 'Gee, he never told me that he was in any kind of danger.' . . . What do they expect? Do they think that Joe is going to tell them what he's been through and what he expects to go through and all the things that he doesn't even dare to tell himself? —Peter Bowman

GI go home . . . before we slit your throat! —North Korean broadcast via loudspeakers into the DMZ

JOURNAL

Sometimes it takes a few visits to win over the infantry soldiers stationed on and near the DMZ. They don't much trust outsiders and are very careful what they say, for fear it might come back to bite them in the ass later. But over the course of a month, I was with the same guys multiple times and eventually they opened up about what was really going on inside the Z. At first, as I listened to their stories, I thought maybe they were just yanking my chain, but I kept hearing the same stories with other DMZ vets, and then I realized it doesn't matter if these stories are true or not. What does matter is that the soldiers deployed there believe them.

$\mathcal{S}$ince 1976 there have been only a handful of U.S. soldiers killed on the DMZ that Americans can recall from news reports—the two officers who were butchered with axes during the unforgettable Tree Incident, maybe the three helicopter crewmen who were shot by an enemy patrol when their chopper strayed over north Korean territory, and the infantrymen on a border patrol who found themselves at the deadly end of a land mine.

What many Americans far-removed from Korea's present-day situation don't realize is that more than 1,200 American, South Korean, and Communist North Korean soldiers have died in clashes since the Armistice Agreement was signed.

NORTH KOREAN WATCHWORDS: DOMINATE AND INTIMIDATE

An excerpt from an article published in *Pacific Stars and Stripes* in August 1976 stated, "U.S. officials believe North Koreans at PanMunJom are under standing orders to use as much force as they possibly can to 'dominate and intimidate' American and South Korean guards." That intimidation often leads to killing American and South Korean soldiers who are patrolling the southern sector of the DMZ and manning sentry posts that overlook North Korea. And shortly after the August 18, 1976, Tree Incident at PanMunJom, Senate Republican leader Hugh Scott stressed that the United States "should insist on condemnation of North Korean barbarism. We should make clear we are prepared to defend ourselves along the border and make sure the next time it is not Americans who get killed in a border foray."

Despite these strong assurances of protection and retaliation from future provocations, there were still frequent occurrences of firefights, ambushes, infiltration, and killing directed against the south and its U.S. allies stationed inside and near the "truce" zone.

Up until U.S. Army units were dispatched further south, every compound between the South Korean capital city of Seoul and the Demilitarized Zone was ringed with concertina wire and chain-link fencing, with armed guards and military police at all entrances, all to prevent enemy intruders from penetrating vital U.S. military strongholds, stealing important documents, and sabotaging the unit mission.

BRUTAL REALITIES OF THE DMZ

Perimeter guards and lookout sentries pulled duty twenty-four hours a day, but sometimes even these security measures weren't enough to deter North Korean agents intent on harming their enemy, "the U.S. imperialists and the South Korean puppet regime."

A young soldier failed to make it back to his unit from an overnight pass in time for morning formation one day. He'd been to the local village outside the compound the night before, checked out the hot spots and back-alley dives, then picked up one of the working girls for a little action.

The overnight surcharge should have included an early morning wake-up call, which would have given him sufficient time to get back to his unit for formation. His buddies had left him in the ville about 10:30 that night—they didn't have overnight passes so they had to get back inside the gates before the 11:00 curfew. None of his friends had seen or heard from him since then.

Later on that morning a local Korean villager spotted the tardy soldier . . . hanging limp from a tree on a hillside overlooking the town. A makeshift noose was used for the lynching. No one really knows who killed him or why. It could have been a drug- or sex-related slaying, but it could also have been compliments of Joe Chink, because it happened only a few miles from the DMZ and it was common knowledge that enemy agents were abundant near every American compound. They also frequented local village nightclubs where GIs hung out.

"GOD BE WITH YOU"

A squad of infantry soldiers from the 2/9th Manchú Battalion waited impatiently for their platoon leader to finish his daily morning spiel that they could almost mimic verbatim. They headed out on a daylight patrol, between the Southern Barrier Fence of the DMZ up to, but no further north than the MDL.

The lieutenant's briefing had nothing new added, "The North Koreans possess the capability to conduct hostile operations against US/ROK forces, in force or in small unit ambushes. The most probable cause of enemy action is continued infiltration through the DMZ. Rules of engagement: Shoot all unidentified individuals who are between the MDL and the south barrier fence, day or night, unless (they are) obviously trying to surrender or defect. Any questions? I'll back tonight," he concluded. Then as an afterthought the lieutenant always added, "God be with you." And the squad always chuckled to themselves, knowing that God doesn't have much influence inside the Devil's Playground.

The patrol had a quiet, yet always cautious walk that day—until they were less than half a mile from their compound on the return trip. It was almost 1800 hours and the sun was struggling to stay on the horizon for a few more minutes.

Always alert, the squad leader spotted something odd less than fifty yards off and he froze immediately mid-stride. The rest of the squad reacted the same, though they hadn't yet seen whatever was out there. The squad leader scanned the area with his binoculars, radioed his position back to battalion headquarters, then approached cautiously, wondering, "Are we walking into an ambush?"

There, sticking out of a nearby rice paddy, casting a shadow like a giant redwood, was a bloated forearm and hand. One of the squad's buddies, who everyone thought had gone AWOL during guard duty a few days before, was pulled out of that field. He'd been found wearing complete combat gear, including his M-16 rifle, helmet, gas mask, and a bayonet in his back.

IF I DIE BEFORE I WAKE

Tension and fear of the ever-impending invasion from the north concerned everyone stationed near the DMZ, so a prankster was often a welcome change. But one morning, what some soldiers thought was a practical joke, turned into total horror.

First call, when the night sentry woke everyone up, was at 5:30 a.m., but at that hour of the morning few of the sleepy-eyed soldiers got up right away. Even at 6:00 some of them were still in their bunks, but once the lights were flipped on, everyone knew it was time to crawl out of their bunks and play army again.

One soldier didn't get up though. Draped over his bunk was a North Korean flag, which his buddies thought was inappropriate, but still several laughed. After a few minutes of joking, one soldier nudged his sleeping cohort, but he just lay still.

The flag was pulled away, revealing a wide-eyed, open-mouthed dead soldier, his head in a pool of blood, his throat slit.

It was one thing, an all-too-common thing, for soldiers to be killed while on a patrol. At least then they anticipated ambushes from enemy infiltrators, but when one of their own died in a nearby bunk, when his throat was slit from ear to ear during the night within a secured compound, it created a sense of helplessness among the other infantrymen.

Again, no one really knew exactly how or why he died. Drugs? Jealousy? Or Joe Chink? But whatever the reason, very few soldiers in that unit slept soundly for the rest of their stay after the incident.

TALKING ABOUT JOE CHINK

A squad of 2nd Division soldiers on a daylight patrol inside the DMZ stopped at a fortified hilltop bunker for a five-minute break. (Nearly every over-watch position in Korea was a maze of man-made trenches and concrete bunkers complete with camouflaged machine-gun nests and surrounded by Claymore mines pointed outward.) Normally the patrol remained silent, listening for any

JOURNAL

Sometimes we had escort duty, and I got the shit detail, babysitting a national print journalist or a bobble-head television pretty boy looking for an inside scoop on the DMZ. I stood off to the side, watching, listening, ready to stop the interview if his line of questioning strayed into classified topics, such as nukes in country. It's always fun to watch the soldiers with journalists eager to lap up every juicy morsel, and the more furiously they jot down every word, the more outlandish the stories get. Sometimes they figure it out, most times they don't. The advantage I had was that whenever the soldiers gave me a specific date and location, I could verify it by checking with the tactical operations center at Division HQ. Of course the official version might not be anything like what I had overheard.

The lookout post at Guard Post Ouellette is only a few feet from the MDL. In the dark of night, North Korean soldiers can sneak close and, without even crossing the border, sometimes throw rocks at the plywood and sand-bagged hut.

It is also rumored they have snuck onto a U.S. compound near the DMZ and killed an American soldier while he was sleeping. Photo by Gary L. Bloomfield.

unusual noises that could mean enemy infiltrators in the area, but an American journalist was out with them on this particular mission and wanted to know the "inside scoop" about the realities of any incidents along the border.

"Okay guys, we've all heard the rumors, but you're the ones who are up here every day. Now what's going on?" The reporter asked. "No more gossip or exaggerations, just tell me what you know."

At first the group of soldiers just remained silent, glancing to see who would open up first, but with more persuading: "Don't worry, I'm not gonna use anyone's name, so you won't get in trouble for anything you say." Still no one said a word, until he put his notebook away. Just to ensure their anonymity they asked him to turn around, facing away from them so he wouldn't see who was talking, and possibly remember their name tag to jot down their comments later. He finally broke through the communication barrier, and soon the young soldiers were revealing what they knew about the DMZ and those things that go "click" in the night.

"Joe Chink often ties dead animals to the MDL markers as a signal to tell us that another American or South Korean soldier has been killed somewhere along the Z. That way we can send out search patrols to find them. Otherwise it might be weeks before one of the regular patrols comes across the body."

"We've heard that soldiers at the guard posts and radar sites are getting their throats cut by Joe Chink hiding in the shadows until our guys fall asleep on duty, and then of course they never wake up again."

"On patrol the only time I get paranoid is when they come on the radio and say 'Joe Chink is out tonight' [meaning North Korean infiltrators are suspected in the southern sector of the DMZ]. That's when we lock and load our weapons. The rumor is that if we kill one it's a plane ticket home."

JOURNAL

A knock at the door. Papa answers, with momma close behind. An Army officer, with a chest full of ribbons, his cap lined with gold braid is tucked under one arm, stands waiting, head bowed. Stone-faced, solemnly he tells them—

"On behalf of the President of the United States, I regret to inform you that your son was killed while serving his country in South Korea."

Momma breaks down immediately. Papa thanks the officer, then closes the door.

"He never wrote that he was in any danger there," Momma recalls, sorting through his letters for any hint that he might get killed. But of course he wouldn't have told them the truth. They probably wouldn't have believed him anyway, after all, the Korean War ended several decades ago.

The squad leader poked his head inside the door and told everyone to "saddle up," abruptly announcing the patrol had to get back out there. He left without saying another word.

"Were they blowing smoke up my ass?" the journalist asked me, as we drove back to division headquarters.

"I've heard similar stories, just about every time I come up here, but I've never seen any evidence, such as a sitrep or photos."

"What's a sitrep?" he asked.

"Situation report. The on-site commander files a report on every incident and forwards it up the chain of command. I've never seen one and I've never heard anyone at division talk about anything like what you heard—like what I've heard."

"So they're blowing smoke."

"Are you asking me or telling me?"

"I'm asking."

"And I can neither confirm nor deny anything you heard."

· δ ·

Chuseok—Korea's Day of Thanksgiving

JOURNAL

1973: My KATUSA roommate—Hyun Shik—was always looking for ways to accompany me off post, partly so he could get away from Army life, but also because I usually paid for anything we did. Maybe we were taking advantage of each other, but I didn't mind because he showed me things I might never have seen or experienced on my own—such as attending the festivities of Buddha's birthday, going to the Korean Folk Village, camping out, teaching conversational English to local college students, or deep sea fishing at night (where we grilled and ate anything we caught). So one day he asked if I'd like to go on a picnic and spend some time with his older brother, catch up on the past year. Didn't even know he had a brother because Hyun Shik never mentioned him before.

After work I stopped by the Class VI (liquor) store and bought a bottle of bourbon for the picnic. Figured it would be just us guys and I'd rather drink that than Mokolai or So Joo, both of which includes formaldehyde. The next morning Hyun Shik and I ate breakfast in the mess hall, then he left, saying he needed to go to the Korean café for something else. He came back an hour later with bento boxes—or whatever they're called in Korean—in a plastic tote. I packed my camera bag—which included my Nikon and a Nikkormat, assorted lenses, a flash, film and batteries, and the bourbon bottle inside. Before leaving the compound, he had to stop by the KATUSA duty office and sign out, saying he was accompanying me on an assignment for the newspaper, though I had no idea what that "assignment" was. I figured it was just his excuse to get off post.

We walked out the side gate and caught a city bus and got off at the National Cemetery, which I thought was a little odd for a picnic, but then I noticed numerous families were queuing at the entrance, and they all had picnic baskets, totes, ice chests, and so on. Hyun Shik just smiled, knowing I was stumped.

"So where's your brother?" I asked, looking around for anyone roughly our age.

"He's already here . . . waiting for us."

Maybe I should have picked up on that subtle clue, but I didn't. What transpired over the next few hours turned out to be my most memorable day in Korea, and I shot some of the most poignant photos ever in my career as an Army photojournalist.

On the fifteenth day of the eighth month of the lunar year, Koreans celebrate the Harvest Moon Festival, known as Chuseok. It is one of the most important days of the year, as families come together to share stories and remember their ancestors. During a trip to the cemetery, a variety of delicacies, spirits, and fresh flowers are laid out to share with the deceased. Some light a candle

Her son volunteered for Vietnam, for the bonus entitlements that would make her life better. She prayed every day while he was gone, serving with the Capital Mechanized Infantry Division, the "Tigers." During the battle near Phu Cat Air Base in late January 1968, the Division killed nearly 280 North Vietnamese. He was one of the few ROKs who were killed during the week-long battle. She stops by his grave three times a year—on his birthday, on the day he died, and Chuseok. Photo by Gary L. Bloomfield.

or incense. A few set up a portrait of their loved one and spend the day bringing them up to date on family activities since their last visit.

An elderly mama-san curses an enemy soldier she's never seen for taking the life of her husband more than twenty-five years ago. Several gravestones down, a group of teenagers are singing folk songs. School girls place flowers by the graves of the forgotten. Small children play hide and seek among the stone markers and no one scolds them. A Vietnam vet shares a bottle of Soju with a fallen buddy.

It's been more than twenty-five years since he came back from fighting up North, the only one of his brothers to make it home. He's told the stories so many times, no one wants to hear them anymore, except his brothers, all three of them buried at the National Cemetery. He's tired and hoping to join them soon. Photo by Gary L. Bloomfield.

JOURNAL

Hyun Shik and I walked slowly along the gravel path, then stepped into the grass and walked between the headstones as he checked the names. "I forget sometimes exactly where they are," he admitted. We back track a few times then he said, "there it is," and we stopped at the grave of his brother and his mother.

She never knew her father. He died in Vietnam before she was born. She's been to the cemetery four times while her mom talks to him about her. She sat there in the grass for ten minutes, pouting, and didn't want her picture taken. I held the camera steady, just waiting and she stubbornly held out and refused to smile. Then I looked away to see if maybe there were any other children and she started giggling, and that's when I took the photo, while looking away from her. A few days later I sent the photo to her mom, so she could show her husband how adorable his daughter had become. Photo by Gary L. Bloomfield.

"He fought with the White Horse Division—the 9th Infantry Division—in Vietnam." He sat down in the grass and pulled out a portrait of his brother in uniform and his mother. "He was killed in Tuy Hoa Province in July 1967, Operation Hong Kil Dong." He opened the bento boxes and placed two at the base of the headstone, then he handed me a box and opened one for himself. From his tote, he pulled out four pairs of chopsticks and a small bottle of soy sauce. "I was fourteen when it happened. My mother cried for six months, then she died of a broken heart."

I hadn't even realized ROK Army forces had fought in Vietnam.

Hyun Shik looked at their photos and introduced us, then he told them about me, and some of the things we did together. I opened my camera bag and lifted out the bottle of bourbon. He smiled, then chuckled, "My mom doesn't drink." I started to put it away, but he stopped me, "but my brother and I do!" We sat there for an hour while he talked to them as easily as if it was a Sunday dinner. We passed the bottle back and forth, though I just sipped at it, while he took swigs, for both of them. My butt was getting sore and I needed to stretch my legs, so I asked if it would be appropriate to walk around and shoot some photos.

"Sure, sure," then he laughed again. "That's our assignment." I left him there to spend another hour with his loved ones, while I walked among the headstones and captured the most heart-breaking photos I've ever shot.

JOURNAL

I returned to the National Cemetery in Seoul, in 1977, for Chuseok and noticed many had lined up to pay their respects to someone of importance though I didn't know who, nor did I recognize the name. I did a feature on Chuseok for the *Indianhead* newspaper and included the following—"Three years ago, Yuk Young Soo was killed by a stray bullet intended for her husband. For most Americans the incident passed unnoticed, but in Korea, the entire nation mourned her death. Even today thousands pay homage to this grand lady, and they remember the work she did for the young, the poor, the elderly. At Chuseok she is remembered by nearly everyone in Korea because her contributions touched so many people. The spirit of Yuk Young Soo—wife of President Park Chung Hee—lives on."

· 9 ·

Tit for Tat at PanMunJom

Sticks and stones may break my bones but names will never hurt me.

No matter how macho a commander may wish to appear to his troops, he should never refuse a chance to sit down or an opportunity to relieve his bladder. —from the Abstract Rules of Combat

In a world full of scary places—Kashmir, Chechnya, the West Bank—the DMZ is perhaps the scariest of all, considering the massive firepower deployed on both sides and the brinkmanship practiced by rival camps. —Reporter Tom O'Neill

*B*ehind the tension of sitting on a powder keg, there's madcap comedy reminiscent of Laurel and Hardy or the Three Stooges that could only be humorous at PanMunJom, the tiny Korean village where two enemies face each other on a border between Communism and Democracy.

Bisected on the MDL that separates North from South Korea is a conference building in the village that has been the site of hundreds of Armistice meetings since a cease-fire signaled the end of the Korean War in 1953. What happens inside that building during "Big Yawn" conferences has worldwide impact, yet most of the stories that journalists on the scene write about deal with the game of "one-upsmanship" as each side tries to outdo the other in minor, yet always image-enhancing ways.

With correspondents from every international news organization, from both Democratic and Communist countries, converging on PanMunJom after every major incident (and any of the minor ones that come to light), it's important for both the North Korean and UN factions to present an appealing and more domineering presence than the other side. And above all, each side portrays its enemy as out-of-control warmongers. This psychological game that seesaws back and forth is a constant battle of wits, nerve . . . and sometimes childishness.

THE TABLE FLAGS

A flag is a flag is a flag, except at PanMunJom.

As a display of national patriotism, two small flags—one North Korean, one United Nations—used to stand at respectable heights on their respective sides of the conference table during the Armistice meetings. But something changed the simplicity of the two small flags, and suddenly they began to grow, and grow, and grow.

The North Korean delegates had noted (after seeing news photos of the two delegations facing off at the table, and after careful measurement), that the American flag stood a little bit taller than theirs, so between one of the

While North Korean and UNC military personnel discuss violations of the Armistice Agreement, the international press looks on and assesses how the talks are proceeding. Because it's important to leave a favorable impression with the press, especially in photos and news footage, both sides play the game of one-upmanship in a variety of inventive and humorous ways. United Nations Command photo.

conferences a one-inch base was added, making their flag slightly taller, thus superior. (Don't forget the importance of appearing more domineering in the eyes of the world press.)

After noticing the difference, the Americans followed suit, also adding a one-inch base to a perfectly stable flag stand, which, because the Stars and Stripes was taller to begin with, made it once again higher than the North Korean banner. Once again the Communists countered the move, which itself was countered, only to be outdone again and again and . . .

The multilayered flag stands kept getting taller until the delegates had trouble seeing their counterparts across the table. Finally, both sides made a momentous agreement to a cease-fire—the two flags would be exactly the same height. No more. No less.

Both flags were carefully measured and matched up. Finally, after months of negotiations and arguing, the two sides had agreed on something, even if it was just a trivial thing like the flags that stood on the conference table at PanMunJom.

But the battle of the flags didn't stop there.

The next day the North Korean flag was again slightly taller than the UN flag. An undetectable piece of felt underneath the base was used to boost it a few millimeters . . . not enough to notice at first sight, but definitely in news photos. Once again the North Korean flag was . . . superior. Tired of the petty game, the UN delegation didn't bother to retaliate in any way by raising their flag again or filing a violation of the truce agreement. The North Koreans had triumphed and trumpeted the victory, and the press corps had a major story to write about!

NATURE CALLS

For numerous sessions during the early years after the Korean War, the Armistice talks lasted for hours, all day and long into the night without anyone calling for a recess or even a short break. Stomachs growled hungrily, and bladders filled to bursting. "Tie it in a knot if you have to, because you're going to sit there and suffer with the rest of us!" stated one delegate from the UN side to a new cohort prior to an expectedly long meeting.

To seek relief from the "nature calls" without disrupting the meetings, many of the delegates on both sides of the conference table brought discreet empty plastic bottles (that would be full by day's end) connected to plastic tubes strapped to their legs and attached appropriately.

At some point though during the history of the PanMunJom "bladder wars," an agreement was reached, allowing for a twenty-minute "nature break" every three hours. Another important decision worthy of front-page news. The bottles and tubes were discarded, but maybe they should have been saved and put on display. After all, they did play an important role in the early decision-making conferences that established the ground rules for today's North/South negotiations.

MUSICAL CHAIRS

Lieutenant Colonel Gaylon Johnson, the commander of the UN soldiers at PanMunJom in July 1975, had countless stories to tell about the North Korean antics in the truce village, but one of the funniest he told has been passed on through the years, and even today an American soldier stationed in the truce village knows all the details about why metal chairs instead of wooden ones are used at the Armistice meetings.

"Naturally enough," recalled Colonel Johnson, "the Americans are slightly taller than the North Koreans. So when both sides first sat down to talk together, the North Koreans found themselves looking up at us across the table. And they didn't like it. (The press reported that American delegates appeared more domineering, in command of the sessions.)

Colonel Johnson continued. "Next time when we sat down, there was something strange. We found ourselves looking up at the North Koreans. They had cut off the legs of all our chairs." Thus the reason for simple metal chairs.

OTHER ANTICS

One of the many North Korean ploys to make the UN delegates appear as "warmongers" involved pigeons.

The Communists decided to paint the roofs of their buildings in the Joint Security Area baby blue, without explaining why. It added a splash of color to an otherwise drab village so no one thought much of it. But, like anything they do, the North Koreans had more in mind than merely giving their buildings a makeover. Secretly, far away from prying eyes, they had painted similar roofs the same color, mixed in with other red-tiled roofs, gray, black, and so on. Then they sprinkled bird food on the blue roofs and released a flock of pigeons, which converged on the free eats. Once they were sufficiently trained, the pigeons were transported to PanMunJom. Then, while the press corps was mingling about, suddenly a flock of birds appeared overhead and descended on those baby blue roofs while they ignored the UN buildings.

"Look," the Communist guards conveniently told the Americans and the press, "even the doves of peace won't land on your buildings."

It took the Americans a little while to figure out what was happening, but once they painted their roofs the same color, the birds landed everywhere. Another international crisis solved.

In mid-April 1969, the American and North Korean two-star generals glared at each other from across the conference table inside the Quonset hut straddling the MDL. The two had been sitting there for four and a half hours without saying one word, waiting for the other to acquiesce and call for a formal adjournment. Four and a half hours. No smoke break or "potty break." Not even just a stand up and stretch break. Finally at 10:55 p.m. the North Korean delegate hopped up and stormed out of the room without a word, and jumped in a waiting staff car.

Without fanfare, Major General James B. Knapp, the UNC negotiator announced, "In view of North Korea's rude conduct, I consider this meeting to be terminated."

IMMATURE BRATS

Years later one MP in the JSA stated, "They send every smart-ass in the North Korean Army down here to spit on our boots."

"It's just completely unbelievable that grown men can behave like this. Some of these men are officers and it's so childish," complained another young American soldier, both assigned as guards for the UN delegation at Pan-MunJom. What he was referring to is the verbal abuse by his North Korean counterparts, which sometimes escalate to stone throwing and other physical confrontations . . . even spitting, biting, kicking are in the North Korean Soldier's Guide to Gentlemanly Behavior!

"We're told not to retaliate, but sometimes, because they act like immature brats, I'd like to bend one over my knee, give him a good spanking, then make him sit in a corner!" This was back when both sides could roam free throughout the JSA, up until August 1976.

THOSE DAMNED FLAGS . . . AGAIN

After the strategic victory over the table flags in the conference room, the North Koreans set out to conquer a bigger, more visible objective—the standard-size South Korean flag that flew at a respectable height over Freedom

Village at PanMunJom. Across the border at Propaganda Village, the Communists hoisted their slightly bigger flag on a slightly higher pole.

And once again the battle was on, and the flags climbed to the heavens.

Soon two metal superstructures supported massive billowing flags at PanMunJom that could be seen poking above the clouds from miles away.

SWEATIN' BUCKETS

In the July 2003 issue of *National Geographic*, Tom O'Neill wrote: "When North Koreans attended a meeting on another occasion with AK-47 assault rifles obviously hidden under their jackets, an Armistice violation, American officers chose not to confront them. Instead the Americans took delight in jacking up the room's heat to equatorial levels just so that they could see their adversaries, unwilling to expose their weapons, squirm and sweat in their heavy clothes."

HUNGER GAMES

Army Specialist Thomas Walker was a military policeman assigned to the JSA in 2000. Among his many duties was protecting the villagers at Taesong-Dong in the southern sector of the DMZ during harvest season. "During one security assignment I was providing security for a group of men who lived in Taesong-Dong, TSD, and were harvesting the rice paddies. During one break, the men invited me to join them while they enjoyed a roasted pig meal on the DMZ, all while under the watchful eye of KPA soldiers. We all sat in a circle and the KPA guards could see us in plain view. I remember one of the Korean men gave me a knife which I used to cut the meat. I would estimate the KPA guard towers were no more than seventy-five yards away. It was a truly surreal experience. I recall KPA soldiers peering from their guard towers while holding automatic weapons. I remember the farmers never being fazed by the KPA soldiers." (It was well known that millions of North Koreans were starving and might get to eat a small portion of meat once a year if they were lucky, and so it was a display of arrogance and superiority for the South Korean farmers to invite their American guardians to eat pork and ham in clear view of the North Korean guards just across the MDL.)

"During another security detail at TSD, I remember being invited to lunch and driven in a Kia Bongo to a family's home in the village. As I sat on the floor with my boots removed, a woman brought in a traditional Korean meal and placed it on a table which could have been no more than two feet high. I remember the traditional staples of a Korean meal, which included rice, were on the table. I was only given chopsticks and no other utensils. After a few minutes of this family smiling and snickering at the sight of me trying to eat rice with chopsticks, a woman brought me a fork. However, it was a baby fork. A member of the family told me this was the only fork they had available in the house for me to use. They even gave me ketchup. The laughter we shared during this moment is something I will always remember. I will always remember the people living in TSD as being some of the most kind and generous people I have encountered."

WHAT NEXT IN THE JSA?

In a desperate move to show the world that even sentry dogs south of the DMZ yearned for better treatment in the north, the Communists employed bitches in heat to entice the UNC canines to "defect." Deadly snakes have been thrown at UNC vehicles, gas tanks have been clogged with dirt, plus a variety of "street punk antics"—such as puncturing tires, and littering the access roads around PanMunJom with shattered glass and metal shards—all well known to the Communist hooligans inside the Truce Village.

To outsiders, the antics at PanMunJom seem humorous, but the American soldiers who live and work there see it a little differently.

Tolerance is a virtue, and for the young American soldiers standing guard at PanMunJom they have to be awfully damned virtuous to survive in that environment.

When North Korea started testing for nuclear weapons, the attitude of the Communist guards at PanMunJom turned even more brazen than usual. Associated Press reporter William Foreman reported in mid-October 2006: "Spitting across the demarcation line that separates the two armies. Making throat-slashing hand gestures. Flashing their middle fingers. Trying to talk to the South Korean troops. North Korean troops in the Demilitarized Zone dividing the two Koreas have been more boldly trying to provoke guards on the other side since the North claimed to have detonated a nuclear bomb.

"They're walking a little taller," Army Major Jose DeVarona told reporters during a tour of the zone. "They're more confident about making contact."

Even before the nuclear equation pushed the tensions closer to the brink in recent years, the antics of the North Korean guards at PanMunJom were just more of the same silliness.

"When we have to go in there every single day and put up with the same BS, it becomes an astonishing battle of nerves."

Barry Sullivan from the *South China Morning Post* best explained the situation at PanMunJom when he wrote, "At the Armistice village the daily scene would be comic, but for the fact that it could one day trigger World War III."

ROUGH DAY AT THE JOINT SECURITY AREA

Stan Suit has vivid memories of his tour of duty in Korea, and especially of one day in the JSA when he ran to help some of his buddies:

"I was stationed at PanMunJom from Dec '69 to Feb '71 as a security guard. I was scheduled off duty when I heard the sound of yelling coming from the center of the truce village. I looked out of a window and saw that two of our guards were being attacked by three North Korean guards, including an officer. I shouted to the other off-duty guards that a fight was in progress and ran to the melee, directly confronting the NK officer.

"I tried to get him to stop his men, but he punched me directly in the face. I hit him in return, and by then the other American guards arrived on the scene. One American came to my aid and hit the NK officer so hard that it broke his own wrist, and sent the NK officer to the ground. The last I saw of him he was crawling away to safety.

"By now more North Korean guards and Americans were involved and our own officer, Lt. James was in the center of it all. He ordered us to back off to the headquarters office, but by now all was in chaos. I and another American were separated from the rest, and barely made it to the back door of the HQ which was fortunately left unlocked. We made it inside as NK guards chased us in.

"Once inside the building, we turned over a table and got behind it for protection as the NK guards were throwing large rocks and construction materials at us through a window. I don't remember the other American's name, but I do remember it was his first day on duty at PanMunJom! What a way to break in a new troop!

"The hardest part was maintaining the situation after the violence subsided. NK guards began throwing construction materials and rocks at us again from what we called the NK Ice Cream Parlor. After several minutes of this, our officer ordered a group of us to attack them, which we did.

"As we charged up the hill to the NK guard post, two NK guards ran out of the back brandishing AK47 rifles. As we got almost to one of them he swung his AK around and planted his feet firmly in the ground. Since automatic weapons were not allowed in the area, this caught us totally by surprise. As he stood there pointing the gun at us, we made a hasty retreat back down the hill to our headquarters building. Miraculously, not a shot was ever fired in spite of the fact all of us were armed with .45 caliber pistols, and the NK with their pistols and AKs.

"One of our guards was almost killed during the fighting when some NK guards dragged him off between two UN buildings and beat him with a shovel, and tried to decapitate him with it. A Swiss or Swedish officer saw what was happening and dragged him into a UN building to safety and thereby saving his life. While my nose was bloodied, the doctor said it wasn't broken.

"Several Americans received the Purple Heart for their injuries and [the severely wounded GI] was sent back to the US. The hardest thing of all was returning to duty facing these same NK guards with whom you were fighting and trying to maintain security." Unexpected? Certainly. Typical behavior from the North Koreans at PanMunJom? What's "typical" is the unexpected.

• *10* •

Tour to PanMunJom

JOURNAL

From the compounds and outposts of the southern half of the DMZ, a distant voice in broken English proclaims the wonders of North Korea, inviting all and anyone to cross over the border and live in a workers' paradise. Surprisingly, since the Armistice Agreement in 1953, there have been very few takers. Off in the distance I can see the Potemkin village of Kijong-dong, better known as the Peace Village, just across the MDL near PanMunJom. It looks idyllic, with blue-tiled roofs and immaculately groomed gardens. And, unlike other villages outside of Pyongyang, it has lights that come on every night. Lights might be one of those take-for-granted luxuries, but a satellite image of North Korea at night is a black void, with only the capital city illuminated. Conversely, South Korea is all lit up, from the DMZ to the southern tip.

Despite the lights, which click on at the exact time every night and click off every morning as the sun is coming up, Kijong-dong is little more than a ghost town, devoid of people, a total fraud to the thousands of tourists who visit PanMunJom, from the southern side of the DMZ.

*T*housands of tourists and business travelers to South Korea are curious to see the most heavily armed border in the world: the Demilitarized Zone . . . a relic of the Cold War. Their first indication that it may not be the typical sightseeing trip is the many restrictions—no shorts or jeans, no sandals, and absolutely no drugs or liquor. During the bus trip from Seoul to the Southern Barrier Fence, they'll be searched and questioned several times, and anyone who jokes around can be hauled off the bus.

97

Often, during the trip north, there'll be singing and jabbering on the bus, but as it gets closer to the border, everyone notices the armed checkpoints, the underpasses and bridges with explosives in place and tank traps (to deter a North Korean invasion), the endless barbed-wire fencing and concertina wire.

A chilling hush passes from front to rear of the bus filled with tourists as it stops at the Southern Barrier Fence leading into the DMZ and PanMunJom further down the road. Only minutes before everyone was joking, saying things like, "Hey, maybe we'll see a North Korean soldier trying to sneak into the south." "Who knows? The North Koreans might be digging another invasion tunnel under us right now." Or, "Do you think one of the Communist guards there will let me take his picture?"

At Camp Bonifas, less than five hundred yards from PanMunJom, everyone is cautioned about what they can and cannot do once they enter the JSA, including joking or taunting or in any way engaging with the North Korean guards only a few yards away, across the MDL.

But after seeing the barbed-wire fence, with its guard towers, minefields, and border patrols, after looking into the eyes of the soldiers stationed there and seeing the seriousness and the fear, the joking on the bus stops and everyone realizes that games aren't played in the Demilitarized Zone, mockingly known as the Devil's Playground, they find out from the driver.

This is where two enemies keep a constant watch on each other, not only with binoculars, radar, and starlight scopes, but also through the sites of American M-16 and Russian-made AK-47 rifles.

The bus is cleared by the American border guard for passage to PanMunJom, and as it meanders its way to the truce village one of the tourists, a self-proclaimed DMZ historian, nonchalantly comments, "I'll bet that even now an enemy infiltrator somewhere in these hills has us sighted with his weapon and is wondering if he should take a few shots just for kicks." Some of the passengers glance out the windows and hunker down in their seats.

The comment only adds to the apprehensive mood as some who might have read something about the DMZ recall previous incidents when North Korean guerrillas ambushed vehicles on this same winding road. It doesn't help either, knowing a tour bus is a much larger and therefore an easier target to hit than an Army jeep.

Some of those news reports they might have read include:

"A Republic of Korea supply truck carrying provisions ran into a Communist ambush near the truce line in which two ROK troops were killed and two others wounded. The incident took place on October 21, 1966, at a point 500 meters south of the DMZ. The Communist armed unit opened up with automatic rifle fire at the truck while entrenched behind thick foliage. In the surprise attack, the driver was killed instantly and as the truck rolled toward them, they kept firing until they thought everybody was dead.

"As the truck stopped moving, a band of North Koreans moved up to the truck and bayoneted their victims before fleeing to the north."

"North Korean troops opened fire on United Nations Command civil policemen who were engaged in checking roads in the DMZ on March 7th, 1973."

"Three U.S. soldiers were killed and 17 others injured when North Koreans attacked a U.S. Army truck in front of Freedom Village on August 7th, 1967."

The tour bus is fortunate, as are the majority of innocents who enter the DMZ—no ambush today—and arrives at PanMunJom unmolested (of course there's always the journey back down that meandering road to the Southern Barrier Fence). Soon after stopping, the tour guide asks everyone to "Please remain in a group and stay within the military police cordon."

There's nothing extraordinary-looking about PanMunJom, other than the wall of security guards that surround all tour groups in the area, but still everyone wants to look at everything and anything because this is where history, both past and present, is made.

The tour's DMZ historian shuffles away from the group and asks a rigidly posed MP in a lowered voice, "Is all this security really necessary?"

The stone-faced soldier replies, "People who like to wander around often get lost up here . . . and some of them are still missing out there," as he

Over the years, PanMunJom has become a popular tourist site, from both sides of the DMZ. A variety of attractions, such as the Reunification Statue, convey a subtle propaganda message. All of the North Korean sites and exhibits blatantly accuse the U.S. imperialists and the "puppet regime of South Korea" for starting the Korean War and continuing the division of the "peace-loving Korean people." Republic of Korea Tourism Bureau.

points toward desolate-looking North Korea only yards away. The historian chuckles, hoping the MP is just kidding, but intent on getting an "inside" look where other visitors aren't allowed, he begs the MP, "Can't I just slip away for a few minutes, to sneak a peek?"

The MP pauses, then pulls out a pen and a piece of paper.

"If you'd like, go right ahead, sir, just give me the name and address of your next of kin."

The historian starts to scribble a name, then scratches it out, wads up the paper, and turns to rejoin the tour group.

"Sir," the MP asks, "why did you change your mind?"

Looking back over his shoulder, the historian explains, "Well maybe there is some truth to the rumor that they don't play games up here. Probably not, but maybe."

As he watches the old man return to the group, the MP mutters to himself, "If you only knew the real story about what goes on here . . . if you only knew."

The dangerous undercurrent along the DMZ is sometimes hard to comprehend when reporters have dubbed PanMunJom "a military theme park" and "DMZ Disneyland."

• 11 •

The Longest, Loneliest Christmas

JOURNAL

December 21, 1979. The worst place anyone could be to celebrate Christ's birthday would have to be near the edge of Hell. Soldiers of the 2nd Infantry Division have a better name for the Hell they have to endure for twelve long and lonely months . . . The Devil's Playground. But the Demilitarized Zone between North and South Korea could hardly be called a playground. Hell, yes, but never a playground. Two years ago I spent my Christmas in that Hell, looking across the Military Demarcation Line into North Korea where they believe in a different god, and Christmas Day means nothing to them . . . except that it's the best time to catch the Americans and South Koreans off guard.

DECEMBER 25, 1977

I filed the following report for the Indianhead newspaper.

For the men from elements of the 2nd Battalion, 17th Field Artillery; lst Battalion, 32nd Infantry; and 2nd Battalion, 9th Infantry, December 25, 1977, is unanimously the longest day they've ever known. From December 13 to the 28 this handful of 2nd Division soldiers man the remotest corner of the world . . . Guard Post Ouellette inside the Demilitarized Zone.

Located only a few yards south of the Line of Demarcation, Ouellette sits on a desolate hilltop dotted with Claymore mines. Fringed with rusty barbed wire, it's an intricate maze of tunnels leading to machine-gun bunkers and lookout posts.

There's not much there . . . an observation room, bunkhouse, mess hall, the tunnels, a lot of sandbags, the barbed wire and those ever-present Claymore mines.

Any attempt to cover up the combat atmosphere by decorating for the holidays only reminds everyone of what they're missing, and where they'd rather be.

To ease some of the tension they usually joke about what would happen if the North Koreans invade the south? But on Christmas Day the reality of being away from home hits too hard for humor.

Adding to that sobering reality is the sound of distant artillery firing from across the DMZ. Those North Korean guns could just as easily be pointed south, and the possibility of dying on that hilltop in the middle of no-man's land haunts every man—enlisted and officer, American and South Korean that serves a few-week stretch any time of year at Ouellette. But during the holidays, the thought of never seeing loved ones again creates sleepless nights, and occasionally a few tears. And their comments reflect that feeling:

"Hell, this is my first time away from home. Sure I've cried. I'm not ashamed of that."

"This is easily my most forgettable Christmas."

"The DMZ is the last place I'd like to be right now."

"I never thought about being away from my family until I remembered it was Christmas . . . it hurts."

Some of them completely ignore Christmas. It's easier that way. Others, those who've received packages from home, take time out to open presents, reread Christmas cards and pass around crumbled cookies. It's a simple Christmas that they all can think of more enjoyable ways to celebrate.

For some guys, like PFC David Woodall, Pvt. Robin Poss, and Sgt. James Rocker, the Christmas packages never came and so "it's just another day."

"You can't help thinking about Christmas because of the tree, the decorations, and other guys opening packages." And Pvt. Poss adds, "You can't ignore Christmas because you remember it as a little kid."

Still the humor helps everyone forget. Spec 4 Mark James, the medic assigned to Ouellette, stated in total seriousness, "I'll probably just say a prayer for world peace, then go back to doing my job of burning human waste. We can't let the enemy get anything vital if they invade, can we?"

A sense of calmness settles over this potential battlefield that's somewhere too far away for other soldiers to think about on Christmas Day. But for the men stationed there, Guard Post Ouellette is a harsh reality of why U.S. forces remain in Korea—On December 24, 1977, Christmas Eve, they all gathered in the bunkhouse as SPC Bobbie Evans, NCOIC at Ouellette said a short prayer, "Even though we are away from our friends and family, we know that they are well, and that God will take care of our loved ones."

DECEMBER 21, 1979

The GIs who spent their Christmas on the DMZ two years ago have all left that hell-hole, but others have taken their place, feeling just as lonely and just as forgotten. And for them, Christmas Day will be the longest day they'll ever know.

During another Christmas, decades earlier, Lieutenant Colonel Darrell T. Rathbun penned a Korean War version of the poem "A Visit from St. Nicholas" by Clement Clarke Moore—

> *"Twas the night before Christmas and all through the tent*
> *Was the odor of fuel oil (the stove pipe was bent).*
> *The shoe paks were hung by the oil stove with care;*
> *In the hope that they'd issue each man a new pair.*
> *The weary GIs were sacked-out in their beds,*
> *And visions of sugar babies danced through their heads;*
> *When up on the ridge-line there rose such a clatter*
> *(A Chinese machine-gun had started to chatter).*
>
> *"I rushed to my rifle and threw back the bolt.*
> *The rest of my tent-mates awoke with a jolt.*
> *Outside we could hear our platoon sergeant Kelly,*
> *A hard little man with a little pot belly.*
> *'Come Yancey, come Clancey, come Connors and Watson,*
> *Up Miller, up Shiller, up Baker and Dodson!'*
> *We tumbled outside in a swirl of confusion.*
>
> *"'Get up on that hill-top and silence that Red,*
> *And don't you come back till you're sure that he's dead.'*
> *Then putting his thumb up in front of his nose*
> *Sergeant Kelly took leave of us shivering Joes.*
> *But we all heard him say in a voice soft and light,*
> *'Merry Christmas to all—May you live through the night!'"*
>
> (published in the December 22, 1951,
> issue of *Stars and Stripes*)

"Merry Christmas to all—May you live through the night!" continues to echo across the DMZ, during every holiday season since the Armistice Agreement was signed.

JOURNAL

Two Days Before Christmas: These guys up here at Ouellette, northernmost U.S. compound inside the western sector of the DMZ, eat great. All their meals are trucked in from Camp Liberty Bell, south of the Z. They get larger portions of everything and can go back for seconds, thirds, and fourths until all the food is gone. And to top it off they even get serenaded while they eat, though I can't say much for the background music, which is propaganda speeches by a North Korean with a lisp broadcast from hidden loud speakers across the Military Demarcation Line.

If that's not enough, North Korean artillery units have stepped up their live fire training during the holidays. Their continuous thunder serves to remind us that at any time, especially when U.S. forces could be caught off guard (such as during the holidays), those enemy guns could just as easily turn south and aim at American targets, such as Ouellette and Liberty Bell, and devastate the unsuspecting American soldiers at each compound.

Merry Christmas and Happy New Year.

The holidays in 1952 were just as cold and lonely and maybe a little more dangerous than every year after for American soldiers stationed along the DMZ. Army Signal photo.

In December 2010, Erich Weingartner with 38North—a project of the U.S.-Korea Institute at Johns Hopkins School of Advanced International Studies—wrote, "after years of refraining from a practice that had irked the North, ROK officials (protected by a contingent of South Korean marines) joined church members in lighting a 30-meter-tall steel Christmas tree covered with 100,000 LED lights on top of the 155-meter Aegibong Peak in Gimpo, Gyeonggi (northwest of Seoul). The 'tree' is visible to North Koreans living near the DMZ, and was part of an anti-cross-border-propaganda agreement reached between South and North in 2003. If the North shoots at the tower, Minister of National Defense Kim Kwan Jin told the ROK National Assembly, 'We'll retaliate decisively to take out the source of any shelling.'"

Merry Christmas and Peace on Earth, Goodwill to all.

• *12* •

Infiltration

One man's terrorist is another man's freedom fighter. —Yonan Alexander

We should build up an impregnable anti-Communist posture so as not to let even a single Communist agent, once infiltrated here, return alive to the north. —Former South Korean President Park Chung Hee, January 1968

JOURNAL

I got in country one year after the Tree Incident at PanMunJom, when two Army officers were murdered while supervising the trimming of a poplar tree in the Joint Security Area.

A year after that everyone was on high alert, knowing that the North Koreans like to initiate provocations on special anniversaries, such as Kim Il Sung's birthday, the signing of the Armistice Agreement, etc. And sometimes they don't do anything, but they like to see us get rattled . . . no, that's not the right word. They like to see us waste time preparing for any contingency. Along the DMZ, any incident can quickly escalate.

As an example, the Tree Incident nearly led to World War III. When the U.S. intelligence ship *Pueblo* was seized in international waters, a variety of actions was considered, including sending troops across the border to rescue the crew, and bombing the port where the ship was taken.

These are just two of hundreds of incidents that have occurred over these many years, and most of them unfolded without any prior warning, which is why constant vigilance is required.

"*I*ntelligence information indicates that North Korea has some 100,000 men who have been rigorously trained for guerrilla warfare," reported the *Korea Herald* newspaper in numerous issues over many years, dating back to the 1960s. "Once they succeed in penetrating into the south they are to pose as ROK [South Korean] soldiers. It is essential to detect and intercept every armed infiltrator before he can perpetrate an act that could hurt [South Korea]. There is virtually no place in the south which is immune to North Korean infiltrators. These guerrillas are armed with poison drugs and poison-tipped needles for use in killing themselves in case they are captured. These 'shock' troops are constantly told by their superiors to kill themselves in case of capture by our security forces."

These excerpts from the mid-seventies reveal that North Korean agents were continually attempting to infiltrate the South—a practice that's been going on for decades.

During the Korean War, weeks before China came to the aid of North Korea after near-defeat at the hands of UN forces in the early 1950s, the UNC suspected, but discounted the possibility of the Red Army entering the conflict. What South Korea and its allies hadn't detected was the infiltration of "some 250,000 men from Manchuria into North Korea . . . completely deceiving the UN Command as to their numbers and positions," reported Gerard Corr in *The Chinese Red Army*.

He went on to report that the Chinese soldiers had moved into North Korea at night and remained concealed during the day, moving forward cross country, avoiding roads to mask any trace of their presence. They infiltrated local villages and dressed like peasants. Thousands more remained hidden in local wooded areas, abandoned mines, mountain caves, etc. Daily UN reconnaissance flights "failed to detect any signs of large bodies of troops, except for known North Korean units attempting to re-group." Soon afterward, hordes of Red Army troops overran the UN frontlines. Eventually the fighting stalled along the 38th Parallel and the Communists stepped up efforts to infiltrate the South with guerrilla troops.

ESCALATING GUERRILLA OPERATIONS

When North Korean President Kim Il Sung established guerrilla training camps in the early sixties, his plan was for "North Korea [to] concentrate its efforts on establishing contacts and bases of operations in South Korea," explained Byung Chul Koh in his book *The Foreign Policy of North Korea*.

Many of these provocateurs were former South Koreans who had been in the north since the Korean War and were sent back home to stir up anti-American hatred and encourage young men to resist the mandatory draft, to persuade workers to strike against unfair conditions and for all South Koreans to lash out against the American aggressors occupying their homeland. Though their stance was pro-Communist, their tactics were not violent, for the most part. But, Byung noted, "in the latter half of 1965, North Korea began to resort to guerrilla tactics on an increasing scale."

The Area Handbook for North Korea went on to report that "in 1966 a decision was made to launch a more active and risky North Korean campaign in what turned out to be a four-pronged operation. The campaign was designed to establish guerrilla bases, to organize underground political connections, to disrupt the South Korean economy and destabilize the political scene, and to lend fraternal support to North Vietnam by diversionary actions in South Korea."

The handbook revealed that, by the following year, North Korea vastly increased its military budget (though it was earmarked more for offensive purposes) "and thereafter stepped up its subversive operations along the Demilitarized Zone and inside South Korea."

TRAINED TO KILL AMERICANS
WITH THEIR OWN WEAPONS

For the North Koreans infiltrating the south, they trained with U.S. weapons so they would be familiar with the same equipment used by the ROKs. The reasoning was simple: "To obtain guns, kill the policemen and soldiers who have them," reported John Barron in his book KGB, the Secret Work of Soviet Secret Agents. "To obtain money, rob banks and stores. While sustaining you, these assassinations and expropriations contribute to the terrorization of the enemy."

North Korea trained hundreds of commandos for missions of spying, assassination and all-out terrorism in and against the south. Many would succeed in their missions, though South Korean and American intelligence sources could not pinpoint just how many enemy agents were believed to have infiltrated the south, waiting for orders to carry out their mission.

AUGUST 15, 1974

He entered South Korea with a stolen Japanese passport, smuggled a disassembled revolver inside a gutted transistor radio, and checked into one of the ritziest hotels in Seoul, playing the role of a Japanese diplomat.

On the morning of August 15, 1974, twenty-two-year-old Mun Se Kwang arrived at the National Theater in Seoul in a rented limousine, a ploy that got him through the usually tight security arrangements.

While President Park Chung Hee was delivering a commemorative address to a packed audience for Korean Liberation Day, the young North Korean sympathizer rushed the stage, firing several shots at the president, who was protected by a podium made of quarter-inch bulletproof steel.

Two bullets strayed though during the exchange of fire between the assassin and the presidential bodyguards, killing a high school girl sitting in the first row of the theater. The other bullet struck the head of the president's wife, Yuk Young Soo, who was sitting unprotected behind the chief executive. That evening, eight hours after the assassination attempt, the beloved First Lady died.

As word got out that Mun Se Kwang had help from two Japanese sympathizers, South Koreans mourning the First Lady's death protested outside the Japanese Embassy. Local police used tear gas to repel the crowds.

MAINTAINING CONSTANT VIGILANCE FOR INTRUDERS

Other infiltration attempts occurred all too frequently during the 1960s and 1970s. The sign at the main gate of the U.S. 2nd Infantry Division's Camp Pelham near the Demilitarized Zone states, "Information on North Korean agents is welcome here." And an Army Joint Message form dated June 1975 pointed out that "the period from June to September of each year has historically been a period of increased North Korean activity in South Korea."

"All personnel must be particularly watchful for any unusual activity." To further stress that point, former 2nd Infantry Division commander, Major General David E. Grange explained to his subordinates in April 1979, "I know you are well aware of the North Korean light infantry brigades who are formidable airborne commandos whose mission is to drop from the sky or emerge from tunnels, or even come in by sea, to attack and destroy ammo dumps, motor pools, fuel supplies and headquarters complexes.

"There are many installations of this type in the 2nd Division that are certain to be on the North Korean target lists. No other division in the U.S. Army faces the immediate and continuous threat of combat that we face here in Korea." Similar cautionary statements and bulletins are issued by every American commander in South Korea, especially those north of Seoul, where enemy activity is most prevalent.

Two American soldiers detected an infiltrator when he set off a trip flare. The GIs threw hand grenades and fired several rounds. The North Korean responded with two grenades. A strike force from the 1st Battalion, 31st

American soldiers along the DMZ maintained constant vigilance, watching for enemy activity, even for this soldier positioned at the Southern Barrier Fence. Photo by Gary L. Bloomfield.

Infantry found the agent's body, plus a submachine-gun. Later that month division troops killed four more North Korean soldiers trying to cross the border and enter Warrior (2nd Infantry Division) country.

A river patrol from the 1st Battalion, 38th Infantry encountered an infiltrator trying to cross the Imjin River only two hundred meters from Freedom Bridge in PanMunJom. The spy, wearing only a pair of swimming trunks, water wings, and an equipment bag with hand grenades, was spotted by the boat's searchlight at 9:20 p.m. The patrol leader at first thought he'd spotted a buoy, but closer investigation revealed it was a man struggling to get away. Ropes were thrown but he avoided them. The patrol leader then tried to lasso the infiltrator and drag him ashore, but that also failed. While struggling with his cumbersome equipment bag, the infiltrator managed to get to the shallows then held up a grenade. The river patrol opened fire before he could throw the grenade, and his bullet-riddled body disappeared as it drifted downstream.

DISPLAYS OF BRUTALITY

That hatred for Americans and even South Koreans is further instilled in the North Korean military, especially among commandos. In early November

1968, 120 North Korean guerrillas came ashore along the East Coast, raided a local village, then rounded up everyone, stabbed one man to death and crushed his head with heavy rocks, as a warning to the others.

American and South Korean forces were cautioned to be on the lookout for enemy infiltrators, and at PanMunJom, the North Koreans were warned to curtail their provocative incidents.

"Whenever and however North Korean soldiers, armed agents or other marauders cross the Military Demarcation Line or land on shores of the Republic of Korea," responded Major General Marvin Demler, senior member of the UN Military Armistice Commission in 1967, "they will be hunted down and killed or captured."

Trained homeland militias in every South Korean village, especially coastal communities, kept a constant lookout for newcomers to their area. In fact at one village on the island of Cheju along the southern tip of Korea, a sign was posted, warning of intruders: "If a stranger spends much money, has no job, doesn't know the exact price of things, and says 'tongmu' (friend or comrade)—grab him! He's a spy."

Crossing the MDL under cover of darkness or through an as of yet undetected tunnel, and landing on a remote coastal area of South Korea, remain the most viable approaches, though some agents slip into the south by swimming the Han River, or by posing as tourists from Japan.

"UNDERGROUND" PERSUASION

Penetrating enemy lines and creating a clandestine fighting force of local partisans is an essential factor in winning a battle. North Korea has made every effort to establish an army of "moles" and instigators in the south. During the fifties and sixties more than four thousand North Korean operatives had been intercepted and arrested, and it was unknown how many others successfully made it to the south and remained in country. Their targets of opportunity in the late sixties became college students and the intellectual elite, both in South Korea and abroad, and in the seventies they attempted to influence academia and the clergy, instigating anti-American dissent.

A good example is the 1980 student demonstrations in Kwangju that quickly turned into an insurrection that had to be put down by armed force. During the days leading up to the protest, North Korean radio bombarded the airwaves with anti-American rhetoric. South Korea also intercepted message traffic from Pyongyang to agents in the south which clearly indicated knowledge of the Kwangju incident.

Several spy rings were uncovered in the mid-seventies, including one with private businesses and spy ships on Ullung-do and another targeting defense plants at Imja-do, both South Korean islands.

U.S. AMBASSADOR TO UN SPEAKS OUT

Since the end of the Korean War and through the 1980s there have been lulls and escalations in the infiltration attempts but they have never ceased all together. While most of these skirmishes rarely make the evening news or the front pages, they are hardly unknown. Three such incidents which occurred in April, May, and June 1978 were presented to the UN Security Council by U.S. Ambassador Andrew Young in a letter dated February 21, 1979 (UN document S/13113), and excerpted here:

"On 28 April 1978, a Republic of Korea naval S-2 aircraft discovered an unidentified vessel making suspicious manoeuvres in the water contiguous to the Republic of Korea, off the island of Ku-do. The naval aircraft notified two Republic of Korea naval patrol boats of the suspicious boat and requested that they investigate. When the patrol boats approached the unidentified ship, the latter opened rocket and automatic weapons fire without warning or provocation. The Republic of Korea patrol craft returned fire in self-defence [*sic*]. In the ensuing exchange of fire, the hostile vessel burned and sank two nautical miles north of the Republic of Korea island of Mun-Do. The bodies of three crewmen from the hostile vessel and the equipment recovered showed conclusively that the hostile vessel was in fact an armed North Korean boat.

"On 19 May 1978, another unidentified vessel intruded into the water contiguous to the Republic of Korea, 2.5 nautical miles off the east coast and some 39 nautical miles south of the Military Demarcation Line-Extended. When the unidentified vessel ignored various signals, the Republic of Korea naval vessels fired warning shots well forward of the bow. Instead of heaving to, the unidentified vessel fired back . . . with both small arms and automatic weapons. In the ensuing exchange of fire, the unidentified vessel was sunk and eight surviving crewmen were rescued.

"On 27 June 1978, another unidentified vessel intruded into the waters contiguous to the Republic of Korea to a point 1,000 yards off the coast of the island of Paenyong-do. The unidentified vessel did not respond to challenges, and due to adverse weather conditions, a collision occurred between the unidentified vessel and a Republic of Korea naval vessel. The unidentified vessel capsized and sank and the Republic of Korea navy vessels rescued five North Korean crewmen."

In piecemeal fashion, hundreds of Communist-trained guerrillas have already demonstrated their irregular warfare tactics against South Korean targets, and "we've seen enough of them through their periodic forays into South Korea," added General Stillwell, "to be aware of their fanaticism and their dedication."

That fanaticism and dedication applies, not just to Communist infiltrators in South Korea, but to the entire North Korean populous—men, women, and children who have been indoctrinated by an all-consuming propaganda campaign, which preaches the annihilation of American imperialism. But what causes this unswerving, almost maniacal tunnel vision?

"There is the glorification of violence and armed guerrilla warfare represented by the romanticized depiction of the life of Kim Il Sung in the media, the arts, including the theater and literature to the point where it seems almost a warrior-leader cult," reported the Korean National Unification Board. "Foreign dignitaries visiting Pyongyang are taken to Moranbong Theater for a performance of 'Sea of Blood,' [which depicts] workers during rest period around one who reads aloud of the glories of Kim Il Sung's guerrilla days: peasants march to gather the fields to military songs and children wear military uniforms to school."

While provocative actions increased in the 1960s and 1970s, then subsided, there have been similar incidents in recent years.

In May 1992, three DPRK commandos dressed in ROK Army uniforms were tracked down and killed at Cheorwon, Gangwon-do. Three ROK soldiers were wounded in the exchange of fire.

In June 1997, three North Korean boats attacked two South Korean vessels. Thirteen months later, a North Korean frogman with a full complement of gear and weaponry was found dead, washed up on the beach south of the DMZ.

In June 1999 and again in June 2002, Communist and ROK gunboats battled in the Yellow Sea, resulting in the sinking of a South Korean ship, and six crewmen dead. An unknown number of North Koreans were also killed. A North Korean torpedo boat sustained damage and caught fire, then sunk with the entire crew trapped inside. Five other DPRK vessels were heavily damaged. And again, in March 2010 the ROK naval ship Cheonan was torpedoed near Baengnyeong Island in the Yellow Sea. Fifty-eight sailors were rescued, but forty-six perished. Initially, it was speculated that the ship may have hit a Korean War-era mine or possibly a North Korean mine, and numerous other scenarios were considered. Forensic evidence eventually pinpointed the source of the explosion as a torpedo North Korea has sold to other countries. Intelligence sources also revealed that North Korean submarines were operating in the vicinity of the Cheonan when it was sunk. North Korea denied any involvement and yet the submarine crew involved in the sinking was later given medals for their "heroism."

Testifying before the Senate Armed Services Committee on September 16, 2010, Kurt Campbell—assistant secretary, Bureau of East Asian and Pacific Affairs, stated: "North Korea's unprovoked attack on the Republic of Korea naval ship Cheonan on March 26, 2010, claimed the lives of 46 South Korean sailors. This attack gave the international community yet another reminder of the unpredictable and enduring threat posed by North Korea. The attack on the Cheonan served as a stark reminder of the importance of our alliance in the face of continued North Korean provocations and raised tensions to a level not seen in many years. This unprovoked aggression reinforces the need to be prepared for a broad range of security challenges from the North and all manner of unpredictable developments. American, Japanese and ROK commitment to the peace and security of Northeast Asia will remain critical to deal with North Korea, but also to ensure a context for peace and stability in the greater Asia-Pacific."

In late November 2010, North Korean artillery attacked Yeonpyeong Island in the Yellow Sea. Approximately seventy houses were destroyed in the bombardment, with several deaths and injuries. New North Korean leader Kim Jong Un had visited with the artillery unit involved, and he was proclaimed a brilliant battlefield tactician. Shelling of the island and the killing of innocent civilians certainly attested to his "military genius."

On August 20, 2015, North Korean artillery opened up on the town of Yeoncheon, north of Seoul. The barrage, according to Pyongyang, was justified because the south had been blasting propaganda broadcasts from loudspeakers at a military base nearby.

THE JAPANESE CONNECTION

North Korean agents in Japan also attempted to "turn" South Koreans living there—an estimated one million—encouraging them to return home to the south and convince their countrymen to speak out against the American occupiers.

In some instances, Japanese citizens were abducted and taken back to North Korea in the 1970s, "to teach language and culture to its spies and to allow spies to assume the captives' identities," reported *USA Today* in September 2002.

For a lot of the detainees, their families and local investigators never knew how or why these Japanese citizens—including women and teenagers—suddenly disappeared. Several have since passed away without ever contacting home. (For many years the Japanese suspected North Korean involvement in the disappearances but Pyongyang denied complicity, until 2002 when Kim Jong Il, in an effort to establish ties with Japan, finally admitted to the kidnappings.)

Many of the younger Koreans living in Japan were born there, but their parents had been displaced when Japanese forces occupied the Korean Peninsula and claimed it as a colony, from 1910 to 1945. By the thousands, Koreans from the northern and southern regions were sent to Japan to work as laborers (in mines, shipyards, and factories). Many of the women and girls became sex slaves for Japanese soldiers.

The ethnic Koreans living in Japan, at least those with sympathetic ties to the Communist north, have established schools which teach Marxist-Nationalist doctrine, idolize the former Great Leader Kim Il Sung and instill hatred for American "imperialists" and its "puppet lackeys" in Seoul. North Korea's policy of "juche" or self-reliance, was very convincing to these displaced Korean citizens yearning to return home and willingly act as agents to further the cause.

The Chongryun, or General Association of Korean Residents in Japan, which has at least 150,000 members (half its total from the 1960s), acts as a quasi-North Korean consulate, funneling vast amounts of money back to Pyongyang (collected from the operation of Pachinko gaming parlors), and issuing visas to these agents attempting to penetrate the south, and to legal North Koreans wishing to return home for a visit.

Some of these Communist loyalists have blended into the South Korean populace, making friends, setting up a business, even marrying to disguise their underlying intentions, only to wait, sometimes for years, for an attack order.

In the March 1969 issue of *National Geographic*, Howard Sochurek wrote, "South Korea. Success Story in Asia." He wrote, "One night . . . I tuned in to Radio Pyongyang, transmitting from the capital city of North Korea. Precisely at midnight a coarse feminine voice announced in Korean: 'I'm going to begin my broadcast. Please find paragraph one of chapter eight.'

"She was referring to the code book used by North Korean agents who had made their way into the South. Two minutes of blaring martial music followed. The choice of tune also gives information to the agents. The voice came on again and, in a deliberate manner, announced, 'Eight . . . five . . . two . . . four . . . one.' Then came a break of three or four seconds, and again a series of five digits. After three or four such groups, she repeated all the digits.

"It felt strange to think that maybe in the same hotel, in the next room, or next house, an agent might be listening to instructions for a new assassination attempt. The slow recitation of numbers continued for ten minutes. Then came another military march, followed again by the five digit code."

That was 1969, at the height of infiltration attempts, but there are still North Korean agents residing in South Korea. The questions continue to haunt, even today: Who are these moles? What is their mission? And when will it be carried out? And how many more innocent people will die in the process?

• *13* •

The Blue House Raid

The guerrilla must move amongst the people as a fish swims in the sea. —Mao Tse-tung

*T*here are no recognizable characteristic distinctions between North and South Koreans, making any enemy agent "just another face in the crowd." Former Chinese leader, Lin Piao, explained just how effective and to what degree partisan fish are allowed to swim in enemy waters. "Guerrilla warfare is the only way to mobilize and apply the whole strength of the people against the enemy, the only way to expand our forces in the course of the war, deplete and weaken the enemy, gradually change the balance of forces between the enemy and ourselves, switch from guerrilla to mobile warfare, and finally defeat the enemy."

Mao Tse-tung simplified the role of guerrilla warfare, which is not to win the war, but to demoralize the enemy by severely crippling him: "Injuring all of a man's ten fingers is not as effective as chopping off one."

That fanatical Chinese proverb was taught to a most-impressionable student—North Korean President Kim Il Sung, who in turn sent hundreds of guerrillas to the south on a "finger-chopping spree." Where and when are the unknown variables that made everyone vulnerable.

Retired U.S. Army General Richard Stilwell, former commander of U.S. forces in Korea lamented, "We wish we knew more about them. So far as I know the north's unconventional warfare forces are probably the largest in the world."

South Korean security officials admittedly warn that "North Korean armed agents are trained to infiltrate into the south by means of gliders, submarines, and boats. This makes our counter-infiltration effort quite difficult."

117

That fact is backed by some very strong evidence—specifically two assassination attempts directed at former South Korean President Park Chung Hee that both came close to being successful, and resulted in the deaths of numerous innocent people caught in the line of fire.

JANUARY 21, 1968

"The mission of the 31 armed North Korean Communist agents who appeared in Seoul Sunday night was to attack Chong Wa Dae, the presidential mansion [known as the Blue House], one of the agents captured alive said," reported the *Korea Herald*, January 22, 1968. Their mission was not just to assassinate President Park Chung Hee, but to cut off his head, take photos of it, and then get back to Pyongyang to celebrate the twentieth anniversary of the Korean People's Army on February 8. Secondary missions, later revealed, were to assassinate the American ambassador and other U.S. officials, raid Republic of Korea Army headquarters to kill high-ranking officers, and blow up Seoul Prison to free jailed North Korean agents or sympathizers and take them back to the north.

The captured agent explained that everyone in his commando group—the 124th Guerrilla Unit—felt it was an honor to be selected for such a glorious task, knowing they would be hailed as heroes when they returned home . . . if they returned home.

Five days prior to the raid, the 124th Guerrillas were taken to the DMZ and issued South Korean Army uniforms, machine-guns, grenades, ammo, and a razor-sharp daggers. That night the unit was led by two fellow commandos familiar with the terrain inside the DMZ. They moved undetected through the perimeter fence despite American patrols and observation tower guards. Brazenly they moved to within a few clicks of the U.S. 2nd Infantry Division headquarters, at the time located at Camp Howze.

But while traversing a tree line in the afternoon, four South Korean woodcutters spotted the commandos laying low in the forest and immediately figured they were Communist infiltrators. They took the woodsmen hostage and probably should have eliminated them, but instead they just threatened to kill them and their families if they told anyone. Knowing how close they were to being killed, the woodsmen promised to keep silent, but almost as soon as they were released, they alerted South Korean authorities.

"Well, of course word spread immediately through the South Korean government and it threw up road blocks, mobilized internal security teams, and covered all the routes into Seoul. But the infiltrators just plain disappeared," recalled Richard A. Ericson, former political counselor in Seoul. "For two days they were not heard from."

The commandos had split up and took separate routes into Seoul, planning to link up at ten o'clock the night of the twenty-first, within walking distance of the heavily guarded presidential mansion. Holding onto the ruse that they were members of the ROK Army 26th Division, the commandos formed up and marched down the center of the thoroughfare until they were stopped at a police checkpoint.

"The police challenged this column and their leader, using remarkably good Korean psychology, told the South Korean policeman to button his damn lip. He said that his men were ROK CIC [Republic of Korea Military Intelligence] returning to the barracks following a search mission. He sneeringly told the police that they should know better than to muck around with the CIC. And, of course, the police backed off," recalled Richard Ericson. "But one of the guys in the police block was a little annoyed by this. He felt it was embarrassing to be talked to like that. So he radioed his headquarters to complain that they should have been warned that there were CIC in the area. The headquarters came back after a while and said, 'There are no CIC in your area.' A police lieutenant on duty at the Blue House heard the broadcast and decided to investigate. He got into his jeep and intercepted the column. By this time it was within eight hundred yards of the Blue House and into a fairly heavily populated area. Seoul in those days was not all that populated to the north; now it is. You couldn't do this thing today. The lieutenant challenged the column and was promptly killed." The commando team scattered, aborting their mission to assassinate President Park Chung Hee, but they turned their vengeance on unsuspecting South Korean civilians.

They tossed grenades at three overloaded buses, machine-gunned passing cars and nearby pedestrians, then hustled into the hills of Seoul. Almost immediately the ROK's Capitol Mechanized Division cordoned off the area and tightened the noose.

"The 2d Infantry Division was placed on alert status," stated the declassified Operational Report of the 2nd Infantry Division for the period ending April 30, 1968. "Operation BIG CLIFF, a contingency plan to counter infiltration and exfiltration, was placed into effect. During daylight hours, units occupied positions offering advantageous surveillance over their assigned sector. During hours of darkness, positions were occupied along roads, trails, streams, and other likely avenues of movement. Throughout Operation BIG CLIFF, close coordination was maintained with Korean National Police in order to control civilian movement."

It took four weeks to track down and kill or capture all but two of the commandos.

"Of the two they captured, one they took to the local police station. Once inside, he managed to detonate a grenade he had concealed on his person, killing himself and about five senior Korean police officials. They didn't shake him down very well, obviously. But the other one, after severe interrogation, broke down and told all about himself and his unit," recalled Richard Ericson. "We were not aware that there were units of this kind, but he said there was an organization of at least a thousand people currently undergoing training in North Korea for just such missions. The Korean military had never heard of anything like this, so they asked him where they had trained. He told where the camp was and drew a map of its layout.

"So we began to believe this guy. He said that their primary mission was to assassinate President Park. They were supposed to deploy not very far from where they had been intercepted, they were getting pretty close. Their idea was to rush the Blue House, raise hell, and kill Park, who was there. He also said that their original mission had been to split into three groups, one of which was to go to the American military headquarters at Yongsan and kill the UN Forces Commander and other senior officers, such as the UN representative to the Armistice Commission. The third group was to come into American Embassy Compound One and kill the Ambassador and anybody else they could lay their hands on there."

Though they failed to accomplish their mission of taking out the South Korean leadership, the commandos still exacted a heavy toll: eight civilians and twenty-six South Korean soldiers killed, plus two U.S. soldiers killed and another twelve wounded. And yes, in Pyongyang the guerrillas were hailed as "heroes" who died for a "noble cause."

Given the relationship that North Korea acknowledged between its own policies and the Vietnam War, "there is good reason to speculate about closer coordination between Ho Chi Minh and Kim Il Sung," wrote Howard H. Lentner in an article, "The Pueblo Affair: Anatomy of a Crisis" that appeared in *Military Review* in July 1969.

· *14* ·

The *Pueblo* Incident

$\mathscr{A}$t the same time North Korean commandos converged on Seoul to assassinate the South Korean President, another incident was unfolding in the Sea of Japan. The U.S. intelligence ship *Pueblo* pulled out of the U.S. Navy base at Yokosuka, Japan, on January 5, cruising through the Tsushima Strait, bound for the Sea of Japan. Her mission was to monitor Soviet Navy activity in the region, intercept radio traffic and gather intelligence on North Korea's military bases along the east coast of the peninsula.

Late in the afternoon of January 20, a North Korean sub chaser was picked up on radar and approached within four thousand yards of the *Pueblo*, which was patrolling in open water. Two days later, two North Korean fishing boats passed perilously close to the ship. Hours earlier, there had been an

While patrolling in the Sea of Japan, the Navy intelligence ship Pueblo *was surrounded by North Korean warships and buzzed by MiG fighter jets, forcing it to surrender and follow the enemy armada to Wonsan Harbor.* Navy History Center.

assassination attempt in Seoul, on the South Korean president, which made international news, and yet nothing about the incident was relayed to the *Pueblo* since it only had one more day before heading back to Japan.

The next day, numerous North Korean warships approached the *Pueblo,* while MiG-21 fighter jets buzzed the ship. Signal flags and radio transmissions ordered her to heave-to, but instead the *Pueblo* headed further out to sea, trying to give the crew time to destroy or dump overboard classified documents and equipment. Warning shots were fired at the *Pueblo*, then peppered the ship with machine-gun fire. One crewman was killed in the attack. Clearly overmatched, the *Pueblo* complied and was escorted to Wonsan Harbor, where the crew was bound and blindfolded and paraded through town, where they were physically and verbally assaulted by the townsfolk.

While the ship never strayed into North Korean territorial waters, according to internationally accepted boundaries, officials in Pyongyang saw it differently.

"On January 23, 1968, the [Korean People's Army] naval ships captured a U.S. armed spy ship, *Pueblo*, and its 80-odd crew members," reported Naenara News. "It had intruded into the territorial waters of the DPRK, or 7.6 miles away from Ryo Island off Wonsan at latitude 39 degrees 17.4 minutes north and longitude 127 degrees 46.9 minutes east, and had been conducting acts of espionage. The ship was dispatched by the U.S. Central Intelligence Agency and equipped with modern and precision radar facilities that could detect the locations of foreign military bases. In capturing the spy ship, the DPRK was exercising its sovereign rights. It was also a natural punishment to the U.S. aggressors, a menace to peace in the Far East and the rest of the world."

Combined with the assassination attempt in Seoul, the two incidents were clearly related, though at the time it wasn't clear as to how. They would soon find out: "The war in Vietnam, by this time, had become a familiar scene to most Americans at home," wrote Army Major Vandon Jenerette in the article "The Forgotten DMZ," in *Military Review*, May 1988. "They watched it on the evening news and grew used to the pictures of bombs, smoke and death that invaded their living rooms. They were informed that we were 'winning the war' and that 'the light could be seen at the end of the tunnel.' Nothing prepared the American public for the events that began on the evening of 31 January 1968, as Tet, the Vietnamese lunar new year, began. It appeared that all of South Vietnam exploded at once when communist forces launched coordinated attacks against US and Republic of Vietnam facilities throughout the country. Nearly every provincial capital and city was hit. The US Embassy compound in the heart of Saigon was the scene of heavy fighting."

"Given the relationship that North Korea acknowledged between its own policies and the Vietnam War, 'there is good reason to speculate about closer coordination between Ho Chi Minh and Kim Il Sung,'" reported

Howard H. Lentner, in "The *Pueblo* Affair: Anatomy of a Crisis," *Military Review* (July 1969).

"The *Pueblo* crisis eventually 'petered out' after the United States decided against any direct action against North Korea. However, there was a substantial buildup of U.S. ground forces and equipment in South Korea immediately following the Blue House Raid. Thousands of troops originally earmarked for duty in Vietnam were diverted to Korea in the first few months of 1968. Along with these actions, a tour extension of soldiers of the two infantry divisions already in Korea helped stabilize things considerably.

"There is reason to suspect that North Korea's original belligerency was a result of collaboration going far beyond its own borders and included players from the Soviet Union, as well as North Vietnam. The timing for the execution of the Blue House Raid and the seizure of the USS *Pueblo* leaves little doubt that they were planned to coincide with communist operations during the Tet offensive [in Vietnam]."

In fact there was a direct correlation between what was happening over the skies of Vietnam and the seizure of the *Pueblo*, but it was more of a payback or "face-saving" gesture. Two years earlier, to give its pilots more combat experience, the DPRK sent a squadron of its MiG aviators to North Vietnam, to engage American bombers. Unfortunately using the same combat tactics from the Korean War, every North Korean pilot, flying North Vietnamese MiGs, was shot down while not one American plane was lost. The "assistance" was costly though to the North Vietnamese, and after two months, they sent the DPRK pilots home, leaving behind the graves of fourteen of their brethren who got a deadly taste of American aviation technology and tactics. Kim Il Sung was incensed at this humiliating display of his military might, and immediately plotted revenge against the United States. The lightly armed surveillance ships that prowled outside its territorial waters seemed like an easy target, and the *Pueblo* became the victim.

South Korean President Park and his council were justifiably concerned that these incidents were a prelude to a Communist invasion and as such, seriously contemplated pulling back their combat units from Vietnam.

"One of our major points of difficulty with the South Koreans was that they thought the Blue House raid, an assassination attempt on their President, was, by all odds, the more important event," recalled Richard Ericson, who was the political counselor in Seoul at the time. "To them, the *Pueblo* was a sideshow. And back in the United States, Americans from Lyndon Johnson down thought that the *Pueblo* seizure was the heinous crime of the century and the Blue House raid was something few had heard about. That became a real bone of contention between us."

On January 25, 1968, the *Korea Herald* reported, "The two incidents signal the beginning of a desperate North Korean Communist attempt at

After the intelligence ship was seized in international waters, the crew of the Pueblo are paraded through the port city of Wonsan, North Korea, where they were physically and verbally abused by local townsfolk and their military guards. Yonhap News Service.

forming a second front in the Republic of Korea to cover up their miserable failure in their futile effort to rally their Communist friends in Asia and elsewhere behind them to set up an anti-U.S. front in conjunction with the war in Vietnam."

President Johnson had his hands full, dealing with the sudden escalation in South Vietnam and considered numerous options, short of war, to resolve the *Pueblo* crisis. He called up the Air Force Reserve and Air National Guard and ordered 350 planes deployed to the Korean Peninsula to bolster his air strength in the region, and counter any air superiority the north might have.

North Korea made the next move in this regional chess match by announcing that the captured *Pueblo* crew would be tried as criminals. This set off a firestorm within the U.S. Congress, some calling it an act of war and demanding a military response, others stressing diplomacy. But Johnson knew, "if we wanted our men to return home alive, we had to use diplomacy. If we resorted to military means, we could expect dead bodies. And we also might start a war."

The *Pueblo* crew was imprisoned for eleven months, subjected to both physical and psychological abuse, starvation, and even threats of execution. When the Red Cross, the press, and foreign diplomats negotiated on behalf of the United States, the North Koreans staged propaganda photos, showing that the crew was being well cared for. The crew reacted with subtle acts of defiance. Displaying the "middle finger" and when asked, they said it was the

Hawaiian hand signal meaning "good luck." But when the photos were released to the international press, the true meaning of the gesture was revealed, which was promptly relayed back to Pyongyang, and the humiliated guards brutally beat the prisoners.

Commander Lloyd Bucher resisted confession to his "crimes" but when he and his crew were threatened with execution, he wrote out a "confession," stating, "We paean the DPRK. We paean their great leader Kim Il Sung," but when he recorded his confession he pronounced it as "We pee-on their great leader Kim Il Sung." Commander Bucher was singled out for especially harsh treatment, suffering kidney and hip injuries, pummeled so often around his head that he sustained a blind spot in one eye and had all of his teeth knocked out.

F. Carl Schumacher Jr., in his book *Bridge of No Return*, who was one of the *Pueblo* officers and during almost a full year of captivity, he and the entire crew was bombarded with pro-Communist propaganda in the form of books, movies, displays, and tours.

Schumacher wrote, "The [North] Koreans constructed a little picture gallery in the foyer of the second floor [where the *Pueblo* crew was being held]. The retouched, out-of-focus photographs . . . portray American atrocities they claimed were committed during the war and then to highlight some of the alleged later incidents. The technique was outrageously contrived. For example, there was a stock Army photograph—one the Pentagon passes out to anyone who asks—of an American tank. The caption read: 'American tank used by Yankee Imperialists in Korea to run over women and children crowded together in a city street.'"

Before being repatriated, the *Pueblo* crew was given a tour of the Sinchon Museum of American Atrocities, the North Korean version of Auschwitz. It is where schoolchildren see firsthand during an annual visit why their entire country hates Americans so much. Schumacher remembers going inside "a large stone building. We took a quick look around this cathedral dedicated to hatred. Here was supposed to be the documentary proof of American butchery during the Korean War. But again, as in all that we had seen, there was no proof at all, merely allegations made through captions on what could be stock photographs from the war. The whole display was ridiculous, in our eyes.

"But at the same time, it was depressing, because we knew that a visit was mandatory for thousands of children in North Korea. It was little wonder that they grew up hating Americans with such intensity."

Eleven months after the *Pueblo* seizure, two days before Christmas 1968, the crew was released at PanMunJom, but only after the U.S. representative signed a formal apology for spying, which he repudiated as soon as the crew was freed.

• 15 •

Other Incidents

"DEEP SEA 129 JUST DROPPED OFF THE RADAR . . ."

*L*ess than four months after the *Pueblo* crew was freed, the North Koreans were at it again, only this time with much deadlier consequences for American servicemen. It was Kim Il Sung's birthday, and the military wanted to do something on a grand scale.

In the late 1960s, the U.S. Navy developed a reconnaissance program named "Beggar Shadow" with the mission of gathering and monitoring message traffic between the Soviet Bloc countries, including its satellites, such as North Korea. A fleet of Lockheed Super Constellations were each outfitted with a full array of radar and surveillance gear. One of these planes—with the radio call sign Deep Sea 129—was patrolling an elliptical loop over the Sea of Japan on April 15, 1969, when it was intercepted by North Korean MiGs and shot down. Thirty sailors and one Marine were killed.

It was a routine flight, similar to ones that had been flown for years, with an established flight plan that would keep them beyond the forty nautical mile perimeter, considered the safe zone.

Rather than deny any involvement in the shoot down, North Korean broadcasts boasted of it, stating the "plane of the insolent U.S. imperialist aggressor army" was "reconnoitering after intruding deep into the territorial air." The attack was a "brilliant battle success of shooting it down with a single shot, by showering the fire of revenge upon it."

Once again, an American president was being challenged, to respond to an attack on U.S. personnel by venturesome North Korean head hunters. At PanMunJom, where the protests and counter-protests were aired, the U.S. delegation headed by Major General James B. Knapp, stated that the aircraft "was engaged in completely legitimate reconnaissance operations" when it was attacked ninety nautical miles from the North Korean coast. "This aircraft was flying a routine reconnaissance track similar to a large number of missions which have been flown over international waters in that area regularly since 1950."

Knapp stressed to his Communist counterpart, "These operations are made necessary by your repeated acts and threats of aggression. So long as such flights are conducted outside your territorial limits, you have no right to interfere with them. At no time did our aircraft penetrate or even closely approach North Korean airspace."

An intelligence report noted that the incident may have been a birthday present to Kim Il Sung, who was born on April 14, the day before the plane was shot down. Pyongyang was still decked out with banners and signs in honor of his birthday, and when news of the shoot down was broadcast in the capital city, everyone celebrated. But soon the chants turned to venom: "Down with the U.S. imperialists."

And several days later, across the conference table at PanMunJom, the Communist delegation merely smiled, daring the United States to respond. No apology, no assurances to avoid future incidents. For the moment, they got off scot-free, walking away from the "peace" table, though thirty-one Americans aboard that plane died at sea.

The bantering at PanMunJom continued without progress, while back in the White House, President Richard Nixon had to deal with his first international incident. Nixon, Secretary of State Henry Kissinger and the National Security Council tossed out all but two options: to order the bombing of North Korean airfields, or continue the reconnaissance flights but with fighter escorts.

According to Nixon's memoirs, Kissinger felt that "a strong reaction would be a signal that for the first time in years the United States was sure of itself. It would shore up the morale of our allies and give pause to our enemies."

Nixon advisor H. R. Haldeman added in *The Ends of Power* that "Kissinger went even further . . . conceding the possible necessity of nuclear bombs as a bottom line if the North Koreans counterattacked."

But with the escalating involvement in Vietnam, igniting another powder keg in Asia would severely stretch American military forces and resources.

Nixon, Kissinger, and other national security members continued to consider their limited options, which included retaliatory moves, such as shooting down a North Korean aircraft, striking a military target in country such as the airfield where the MiGs took off from. This could be done via combat aircraft or naval bombardment. Other options included infantry raids across the DMZ, artillery or missile attacks across the DMZ, a naval blockade, mining North Korean ports and harbors, or seizing North Korean assets abroad.

The North Korean delegation at PanMunJom denounced the U.S. allegations as mere fabrications, a ploy designed to gain world sympathy and support against the "U.S. imperialists and their constant pursuit of continuing the war between the Korean people."

Kissinger later dubbed this initial trial by fire of the Nixon administration as a failure. "Our conduct in the EC-121 crisis [was] weak, indecisive and disorganized."

The U.S. response, or lack of one, would bother Nixon and he would later admit to Kissinger, "They got away with it this time, but they'll never get away with it again."

Bold talk with little or no action to support it, for there have been numerous similar incidents where American lives were lost and the instigators "got away with it . . . again . . . and again . . . and . . . ."

In April 2017, Van Jackson of the Wilson Center's North Korea International Documentation Project, reflected on the shoot down of the Navy reconnaissance plane and how it impacts recent negotiations with Pyongyang. "In today's national security agenda, there is a pressing need to understand North Korea's 'theory of victory'—a term that broadly characterizes what North Korea believes is necessary and sufficient to deter adversaries, secure political goals, and control escalation in a crisis."

North Korea's former foreign minister and deputy chairman of the cabinet of ministers—Pak Seong Cheol—had met with Soviet Ambassador

While conducting surveillance of military activity, a Navy EC-121 spy plane was shot down by North Korean MiG fighter jets over the Sea of Japan, in mid-April 1969. Navy Historical Center.

N. Sudarikov after the EC-121 shoot down, and he repeated a phrase Kim Il Sung had stated many times before, that North Korea is "ready to respond to retaliation with retaliation, and total war with total war."

Van Jackson added, "When Pak [Seong Cheol] was pressed on whether North Korea understood the escalation risks of using violence against the United States, he replied 'we've also shot down American planes before, and similar incidents are also possible in the future. . . . It's good for them to know that we won't sit with folded arms.' Clarifying further, Pak conveyed: 'If we sit with folded arms when a violator intrudes into our spaces, two planes will appear tomorrow, then four, five, etc. This would lead to an increase of the danger of war. But if a firm rebuff is given, then this will diminish the danger of an outbreak of war. When the Americans understand that there is a weak enemy before them they will start a war right away. If, however, they see that there is a strong partner before them, this delays the beginning of a war.'

"Pak Seong Cheol showed a firm belief in reciprocal, automatic violence when attacked, on the grounds that failing to retaliate will cause one to suffer future attacks. When he claimed that small attacks like the EC-121 shoot down help prevent general war, he was arguing that small acts of violence establish general deterrence; they are the 'real' reason the United States does not invade." (It should be noted that aerial and naval reconnaissance far beyond North Korea's territorial boundaries are considered "acts of violence," thus justifying seizing an intelligence ship or the shooting down of a military spy plane.)

"North Korea believes military force has political value, escalation is a reliable means of de-escalation, provocations help deter 'US aggression,' and retaliating when attacked is essential to maintaining credible deterrence. Policymakers must heed this highly offensive and reputational 'theory of victory,' or risk inadvert war."

DÉJÀ VU . . . ALL OVER AGAIN

"In the morning of March 1, 2003, an American RC-132S spy plane, Cobra Ball, took off from a U.S. airbase in Okinawa, and cruised along the East coast of North Korea collecting electronic signals. The US intelligence suspected that North Korea was about to test a long-range missile and the plane was there to monitor the suspected missile launch," stated Han Ho Suk, director of the Center for Korean Affairs, on April 24, 2003. "When the US plane reached a point about 193 kilometers from the coast of North Korea, two MiG-29 and two MiG-21 fighter planes showed up unexpectedly. The

JOURNAL

What is well known is that the United States did and continues to rely on reconnaissance planes and ships prowling close to an enemy's territory to gather intelligence and monitor activity, such as troop movements and in recent years regarding North Korea, nuclear tests.

This surveillance was done along the trace of the Iron Curtain to spy on the Soviet Union and other Warsaw Pact countries, and certainly with North Korea for decades.

SR-71 spy planes have also flown over Communist countries, including Cuba during the missile crisis.

Along the Korean DMZ, U.S. and South Korean helicopters have strayed into North Korean airspace, most often inadvertently, due to inclement weather. For infantry patrols it's very easy to see how helicopter pilots could lose track of the border markers along the Military Demarcation Line. Many are little more than fence posts, often obscured by bushes and trees.

North Korean planes approached . . . and signaled the US plane to follow them. The US pilot refused to follow the command and left the scene post-haste. The US plane was tailed by the hostiles for about 22 minutes but let the US spy plane go."

This incident could easily have been a repeat of the fatal shoot down of the Navy spy plane in April 1969. "If Kim Jong Il had given the command, the MiGs would have shot down the US plane and returned to their base before the U.S. could have scrambled war planes."

BOMBING IN BURMA

In October 1983, South Korean President Chun Doo Hwan and his delegation were in Rangoon, Burma, for an official state visit. It was part of an extended tour of six Asian countries. On the itinerary was a wreath-laying ceremony at a mausoleum near the Shwedagon Pagoda, to honor Burmese dignitaries who had been assassinated by their opponents in 1947. Members of both the South Korean and Burmese cabinets were in place, waiting for President Chun, who was running late. A remote-controlled bomb exploded at the site, killed several of the Korean cabinet members including the ambassador to Burma, thirteen other South Koreans and four local nationals, with thirty-two more critically injured. President Chun's tardiness had spared his life.

Soon after President Chun considered the bombing "a grave provocation not unlike a declaration of war." North Korean leader Kim Il Sung scoffed at the accusation, dismissing it as "a preposterous slander." But soon after two North Korean Army officers were arrested in the Rangoon District Court, and confessed to the bombing. The two were sentenced to death.

THE MASSACRE OF INNOCENT CIVILIANS

Quite possibly the most callous act of provocation occurred in November 1987, when a Korean Airlines Boeing 707, was destroyed midair over the Andaman Sea by a bomb planted by two unassuming North Korean agents. Twenty crew members and ninety-five passengers perished. The two bombers, posing as father and daughter, were tracked down at a hotel in Bahrain. Before they could be arrested, they both swallowed cyanide pills hidden in a pack of cigarettes. The older man died immediately, but the younger bomber, a female named Kim Hyon Hui, survived and later admitted to the attack. Saying the bomb—hidden in a radio, left in the overhead compartment—was smuggled aboard when the plane stopped in Abu Dhabi.

"I had been brainwashed from childhood to believe that it was my duty to die for the leader, Kim Il Sung. And that's all I knew, since the leader is a god. I was indoctrinated to believe that my mission was for the good of the Korean people, and the reunification of our country."

In fact, the primary reason for the attack was to sabotage the 1988 Olympic Games in Seoul. Simple as that.

Though she was sentenced to death, Kim Hyon Hui was flown to Seoul where she was pardoned by President Roh Tae Woo, who felt she had been brainwashed. Because she is deemed a traitor, Kim has been under house arrest in South Korea, in fear that North Korean agents will track her down and silence her. In recent years she has served as an analyst and consultant on North Korean affairs.

DAVID VERSUS GOLIATH

During a 1976 talk with a Japanese magazine editor, Kim Il Sung declared his innocence in the numerous international incidents blamed on North Korea, saying, "Who will believe that such a small country as ours is threatening the United States that is seeking to dominate the world? No people would believe it. And yet the U.S. imperialists and the South Korean authorities persist in their unfounded argument that we are threatening South Korea. Quite contrary is the fact: Not we but precisely the U.S. imperialists and the south are creating the danger of war; we are not threatening South Korea, the U.S. imperialists are threatening us."

Selective memory also plagued Kim Il Sung's son—Kim Jong Il—and may yet infect the inexperienced and unpredictable Kim Jong Un, who is eager to prove he is a worthy successor.

· *16* ·

The Children

Youth is easily deceived because it is quick to hope. —Aristotle

What's done to children they will do to society. —Karl Menninger

The greatest happiness is to vanquish your enemies, to chase
them before you, to rob them of their wealth, to see those dear
to them bathed in tears, to clasp to your bosom their wives and
daughters. —Genghis Khan

The young Korean soldier sat beside the country road, straddling his weapon,
taking a break under the sweltering midday sun. The dust from passing buses
left a gritty taste in his mouth, while a growing sweat stain traced its pattern on
his back. He reached for his cup, hoping to turn the grit into mud, but there
was no water left to drink. He swung the spear back and forth, and his feet had
blisters due to pop if he had to walk even ten more feet.

He'd closed his eyes for what seemed like only a few seconds, but the
footfalls of another soldier fifty yards off brought his mind back into focus.
His whole body hurt from the heat, and the walking, but the ache was soon
forgotten as the young Korean straightened up his clothes and wiped the dust
off his weapon. He even stomped his feet for a quick dust off to impress the
other soldier, an American, now only a few yards away. As his U.S. counterpart smiled and walked by, the Korean soldier snapped to attention and saluted
proudly. The American waved a casual "hi" but his ally responded by bellow-
ing a war cry—"PAWN GONG" (Against Communism).

The action greatly disturbed the GI, not because he wasn't accustomed to
the ROK Army's slogan, but because this particular Korean "soldier" was only
three years old. The boy didn't have to be out there with his spear, guarding

During the Team Spirit war games, involving American and South Korean forces, this boy sat by the side of the road, "guarding" his house. Photo by Gary L. Bloomfield.

his home on that dusty road, but he was practicing up for when it would be his turn to play soldier . . . for real.

American children think of war as a game . . . "Bang, bang, you're dead" . . . then return their guns to a toy box, only to fight another battle tomorrow. But in South Korea, especially north of Seoul, the potential for war is less than thirty miles away. And in North Korea, the children are taught, even drilled on how to hate, how to fight, and even how to kill if they have to. And the enemy they grow up hating the most, are American soldiers occupying the southern half of the Korean Peninsula. In South Korea, the children are aware of the division of their homeland, but they're not brainwashed to hate or kill, like those children in the north.

An excerpt from a UPI article in August 1978 revealed one aspect of North Korean schooling when it stated that "Kindergarten children in the capital of Pyongyang beat the dummy of an American soldier with sticks. One of the children, dressed in the uniform of a North Korean soldier, smashed in the dummy's head."

To North Koreans, young and old, these deeds include a total devotion to their beloved leader Kim Il Sung, then, after he died, to his son—Kim Jong Il—and now that devotion is for the next Kim—grandson Jong Un.

The legend and adoration of Comrade President Kim Il Sung—the father of North Korea—is hard for many Westerners to comprehend. Facts about his fetes could have been accomplished by no one less than a superhuman, for he has been at several places on the same day at the same time; has traveled at the speed of light (or so it is said), and his every word is immortalized, for he is the wisest of all sages.

Kim memorabilia borders on the ridiculous—a clay earthen pot he once "looked into," a pencil he once used, or a straw mat he once sat on.

He is the conqueror, the great leader who stoned Japanese invasion ships, and who once caught a rainbow in his hands, and drove off the cowardly U.S. imperialists from his beloved homeland. This is what the children of North Korea are taught, beginning in nursery school.

They learn how "miserable" their Korean brothers and sisters in the south are treated by the American warmongers, of families separated by the Demilitarized

From a very early age, North Korean children are brainwashed to hate and to kill American soldiers occupying the southern half of their homeland. Korean Overseas Information Service.

Zone, and of the beloved Kim Il Sung's quest to reunify the Korean people, but only after slaying the U.S. dragon that lurks everywhere on the peninsula. With patriotism and dreams of reunification so deeply imbedded in their mind, every North Korean is prepared "to give their life for it." But, stressed Kim Il Sung, reunification can only be achieved by "driving the American imperialists into the sea." The same rhetoric is spewed out now by the younger Kim. (And despite recent agreements between the United States and North Korea, to lessen the threat of nuclear war, and with that the hatred of America, the brainwashing of two entire generations of the populace will not disappear overnight.)

Much of North Korea's military-oriented educational system (in all its bloody brutality and falsehood) is patterned after its most influential big brother—Communist China: "Included are close-order military drill, throwing grenades, and hand-to-hand combat. The teachers are . . . members of the People's Liberation Army, assigned to spread what one calls basic knowledge of military affairs and Maoist ideology," reported Warren Phillip, and Robert Keatley in *China: Behind the Mask.* "Few are too young for some indoctrination. Children can buy toy rifles whose bayonets can be jabbed into paper tigers labeled 'American imperialism.' Even four-year-old girls sing songs about fighting foreign foes. One line goes, 'Sha, Sha, Sha [Kill, Kill, Kill].'"

North Korean defector Choi, Dong Chul, born in the northern Hangyong Province recalled that when he was a teenager, he joined the Son Yun Dan, or Young People's Group and the lessons included memorizing Kim Il Sung's speeches and the central party regulations. Those who remembered the most were rewarded. Indoctrination immersed the students in Communist ideology and those who excelled had an opportunity to go to college. Those who didn't were sent to work in the mines and factories, with no opportunity to improve their standing.

THE DEADLY INNOCENTS

To complement its infiltration strategy, North Korea has established special units of young girls, named Moran units. After training they are sent to Japan, then receive visas to South Korea. These girls dress in school uniforms and hang around parks in Seoul, blending in with other school girls selling packs of gum to pay for their tuition. But the gum these Moran girls are handing out is laced with poison, and they roam the parks looking for soft-hearted American GIs and other Westerners who can't resist helping out these unfortunate girls.

South Koreans know to keep a lookout for suspicious-looking infiltrators, but the Moran girls are especially deceiving.

"All citizens must have the resolve to bear arms and fight the enemy if he comes," stated former South Korean President Park Chung Hee in 1968.

He was referring not only to draft-age men, but women, the young and the elderly . . . everyone must strive to thwart a recurrence of the Korean War, at all costs.

But whether in South Korea or the Communist north, these youth-oriented "sociology" lessons in school, the community and at home have more of an influence on the children who've lost a relative in the Korean War . . . a relative who died years ago, long-before these schoolchildren were even born.

"You must avenge your grandfather's death, by killing his enemy's grandson."

For all-too-many Korean children on both sides of the Demilitarized Zone, they would wait a lifetime to fulfill that dream.

JOURNAL

Christmas Day, 1972: Had a wonderful time at the Tender Apples Children's Home in downtown Seoul. No Santa, no presents, but a lot of warmth and joy. There's a piano in the main hall so while they were eating (rice and kim-chi), I started playing Christmas carols and soon about fifteen of them were crowded around me singing in Korean. It sounded pretty good till I tried to sing "Silent Night" in Korean. I thought I was doing pretty good, but they got quite a laugh out of it.

For Christmas dinner they all had more rice and kimchi and a special treat, half of a baked potato. Nothing on it, like butter or sour cream and chives or even salt. I ducked out to a nearby bakery and bought enough sweet rolls so each child could have one. I couldn't believe how overjoyed they were. They're all so adorable. You can see they want to be loved because they're always clinging to each other.

JOURNAL

June 1977: Went to NamSan Park (in Seoul) today with the children from the orphanage. Always lots of high school girls there selling packs of gum and bouquets of flowers to pay for their school tuition. Price is usually twice as much as a sidewalk vendor, but I always buy at least one pack of gum from each girl who approaches me.

Found out about the Moran units of North Korean girls smuggled into the south to kill Americans and how they often seek us out at parks, selling packs of poisoned gum. I still bought the gum but didn't eat any of it, just tossed it out once I got back to the barracks.

• *17* •

The DMZ's Porous Southern Barrier Fence

*J*n 2003, American troops along the DMZ began a phased withdrawal, relinquishing those frontline compounds and guard posts to the ROK Army. For more than fifty years, nights were the worst for the American soldiers manning the guard posts along the DMZ or out on patrol seeking out infiltrators, though they rarely experienced a firefight. They could hear them out there, North Korean soldiers, in the darkness, the metallic clicks, the laughter and the taunts, but they rarely saw their tormentors. The GIs were given the latitude to fire on anything that moved inside the DMZ at night but often they just fired in the direction of the sound. It was a war of nerves, a game of cat and mouse, though it was hard to tell who's chasing who.

JOURNAL

Galen Geer and I survived the Korean DMZ together—I made sixteen trips there—and we tolerated the 2nd Infantry Division together—though often our office resembled the chaos of *M*A*S*H*. He was the seasoned "grunt" who kept me out of danger whenever we put on flak jackets and helmets. I kept him out of trouble when it came to issues of protocol and diplomacy—such as navigating that minefield known as the Division Command Group. We leaned heavily on each other for a helping hand. We shared the chores of driving back and forth from Camp Casey to the DMZ, we looked out on North Korea from Guard Post Ouellette together, we took turns shattering each other's deep sleep at 0430 in the morning to fall out for PT, we even shared a few stiff drinks together (even though I don't drink), and we walked the Southern Barrier Fence of the DMZ side by side.

I had escort duty, accompanying a nationally known reporter to the DMZ, but before we could pass through the checkpoint at the Southern Barrier Fence, the sentry had to call back to the 2nd Division's Tactical Operations Center to verify that the reporter had clearance to be there. Photo by Gary L. Bloomfield.

JOURNAL

Those who haven't been often compare the Korean DMZ with the former Iron Curtain that separated the communist Warsaw Pact countries from the rest of free Europe. Both "walls" are intended to impede an invasion but the fortifications are vastly different. The Iron Curtain was a solid and towering concrete wall, topped by concertina wire. On the communist side were motion-activated shotguns, a minefield, guard towers, and a high-speed road, all intended to stop anyone from attempting to defect. Work patrols were guarded by heavily armed soldiers. On the western side of the "curtain" were allied observation posts to monitor any potential buildup of enemy forces, but no minefields or any other obstacles. (The deterrents on the east side of the wall would also create a deadly gauntlet for anyone attempting to defect from free Europe to the Communist side.)

The Korean Demilitarized Zone may in fact be the most heavily "militarized" region in the world, but the actual border that separates North from South Korea is little more than a series of disconnected fence posts. The minefields are there, on both sides, and with a little luck, they can be negotiated without personal injury to North Korean commandos attempting to infiltrate the South, or for defectors fleeing the Communist North.

JOURNAL

Galen Geer and I served together with the 2nd Infantry Division Public Affairs Office, overlapping six months—my last six, his first six in country. We were total opposites—he was a heavy smoker and drinker, I was neither. He used every swear word known to GIs worldwide, I knew them too but avoided using them. He was a grunt—combat veteran from Vietnam—and I was a REMF. Total opposites, but somehow we made it work. He was already writing freelance magazine articles back then, mostly for hunting and fishing magazines. Showed me the checks he was getting for published features on making fishing lures, and the best fishing holes for rainbow trout. Made it sound so simple. It wasn't.

Following is one of those articles he wrote about the DMZ, this one for *Soldier of Fortune* magazine, in December 1979.

The Demilitarized Zone is nothing but a slash cutting the Korean Peninsula in half, with North Korean soldiers positioned and patrolling the northern half, and South Koreans, Americans, and assorted United Nations units responsible for the southern half. Down the middle are simple marker posts which identify the Military Demarcation Line, or MDL. Sometimes these markers are covered by underbrush or intentionally moved, and when an enemy patrol strays across the line, even if by mistake, that is a violation of the Armistice Agreement.

The Southern Barrier Fence and its fringes are heavily fortified with minefields, spot lights, motion sensors, chain-link fencing topped with razor-sharp concertina wire, a strip of raked sand (to easily spot the footprints of intruders), checkpoints at every roadway, and those foot patrols.

PATROLLING THE DMZ

> It is a doctrine of war not to assume the enemy will not come, but rather to rely on one's readiness to meet him; not to presume that he will not attack, but rather to make one's self invincible. —Sun Tzu, *The Art of War*

I gunned the olive-drag CJ-5 as I neared the north end of the bridge over the Imjin River. The Red Cross compound flashed past on my left. A minute later the last U.S. Army battalion-sized compound, Camp Greaves, of the First of the Ninth Infantry (Manchus), flew past. I was in a hurry and the other compounds—Four-Pappa-One North, the last active fire base in the U.S. Army, and Warrior Base, a battalion staging area—were blurred by the speed of the jeep.

Past Warrior Base the black, asphalt road turned sharply left, back toward the DMZ, and the lone ROK sentry on duty waved as I passed, his frag grenades worn like badges of honor. Finally I topped a small hill and could see the buildings of Camp Kitty Hawk, the UN Command's home for the military police of PanMunJom, and the gate to Camp Liberty Bell, the northernmost American compound in Korea, was across the road. I turned right and waved to the guard as I drove into Liberty Bell. I had a half hour to spare.

As a military journalist with the 2nd Infantry Division—Indianhead Division—in Korea, I had visited the area of Liberty Bell, the guard posts inside the DMZ and PanMunJom, on several occasions. This time was different; I was on assignment to accompany a civilian journalist on a combat patrol inside the DMZ. Between the two Koreas.

Camp Liberty Bell is the home of Company A, 1/9th Infantry, which normally has the mission of patrolling the DMZ and guarding the short stretch of the fence along the southern boundary still in American hands. During the spring and summer months, while the 1/9th is off in other parts of Korea training, other 2nd Division battalions move north from their camps along the classic invasion routes to Seoul, and establish their headquarters at Camp Liberty Bell. The main body of the battalion lives at Warrior Base in tents built by the Division's 44th Engineers.

The camp is only a few hundred meters south of the DMZ and portions of it are ringed with minefields. In addition, throughout the area, are reminders of the grim reality that is looking at them from nearby hilltops—North Korea. At one end of the camp are bunkers and the ammo dump, ringed with mortar positions. Oddly, a volleyball court is set up between the positions.

I parked my jeep across from the Battalion Tactical Operations Center (TOC) for the 1/31st Infantry (Mechanized) who were on the mission at that time. Walking toward the sentry on duty outside the TOC I carried my flak jacket, .45, helmet, and other gear slung across one shoulder and my camera bag over the other. As he stepped out to stop me I handed him my press ID and stood back to light a cigarette while he called one of the battalion officers to let them know "another reporter" had arrived. Seconds later a burly, mustached major appeared from the maze of tents. Sweat rolling down his face.

"Glad you could make it," he said, extending his hand. We had worked together during other operations in Korea.

He gave me my admission badge to the TOC and walked past the sentry. As we walked he explained that the patrol members had been briefed and the

All vehicles entering and leaving the DMZ are checked at the Southern Barrier Fence before being allowed to pass. North Korean infiltrators have been known to wear ROK Army uniforms and in the past, ambushed vehicles. The guards on duty are on constant alert for hostile penetration attempts. Photo by Gary L. Bloomfield.

reporter was waiting inside the briefing tent. Neither the major nor the men were thrilled about having the press along on a patrol. In the months following President Carter's announced plans to pull the ground forces out of Korea, the DMZ and the American troops have become popular stopping places for reporters. Many of them whom the public affairs office in Seoul, headquarters of Eighth Army, sent up to go on patrol or see what it's like, had proven themselves to be naïve men and women with little understanding of the military or the Korean situation. Some even believed the war was completely over.

"This guy's a little pudgy," the major continued. "I don't know if he is going to be able to keep up with the patrol. I've told them to keep it routine—no fancy stuff. But I don't want them out there after dark, so I hope he can keep up."

I agreed, then added, "My job is to keep him out of trouble and get him out of there if there is trouble."

Inside the briefing tent a 3-D sand mock-up of the DMZ area controlled by the 2nd Division sat on the wooden tent floor. The major quickly introduced us and I caught the name "Jim" and Reuters News Service, the rest of it slipping past me. After the quick briefing, two sets of equipment were brought in, including two M-16s. I declined the weapon and the equipment, preferring my own and the .45 as it allowed me to keep my hands free to use my cameras.

After Jim was fitted with a flak jacket, pistol belt, canteen of water, and first aid kit, the major dug out the camouflage sticks and we went to work painting our faces and all exposed skin. When we had finished the job the major handed Jim the M-16 and asked if he knew how to use it.

"Oh, I think so," he answered, then quickly broke it down into its major groups and reassembled it, while keeping a running conversation going on various small arms from around the world. I smiled at the major; our pudgy reporter was a pro—I wondered who was taking care of whom.

A half hour later we climbed in three jeeps for a ride to our jump-off point a few hundred meters inside the DMZ. (The ride, I believe, was for our convenience.) Our patrol would wind through swamps, woods, rice paddies, over hills and through creeks, looking for infiltrators and routes they might be using. The patrol would move up a hill towards one of the two American guard posts—116—and end at the fence-line of the post.

The squad eyed both Jim and me suspiciously—my cameras and Jim's beard making us both feel conspicuous. Jim and I were treated as if we were intruders into an illegal cock-fight. The entire squad chose to ride together in two jeeps while Jim and I were left with one to ourselves and the driver.

At the fence, weapons were checked and loaded and our IDs cleared with the TOC. Then we were waved through and an eerie silence settled over us. The quiet inside the DMZ is nerve-shattering after experiencing the noise of Seoul and other Korean cities. As we rode I pointed out the signs along the road warning of minefields. There was no doubt where we were.

As we rode past a field of rice paddies, Jim pointed out the birds (cranes and white egrets) that had found a refuge inside the DMZ and said he planned to write an article about it, explaining that it was ironic that the combat zone between two countries still legally at war was a wildlife refuge where leading naturalists came to study endangered birds.

The lead jeep turned off the paved road into a narrow, rut-torn, abandoned road that wound through several stands of trees. Near a bridge still bearing the scars of war we stopped and piled out. After the jeeps had turned around and left, the patrol members quickly fell into position, with Jim and me near the center of the patrol, and moved out.

Both the U.S. and South Korean military maintain day and night patrols in the southern half of the DMZ. The patrols are important intelligence-gathering efforts for the 2nd Division and UN Command as well as the South Koreans. The patrols often discover new signs of infiltration by the North and periodically night ambush patrols become involved in quick fire fights. Day patrols are usually for recon only, to gather information, while night patrols are sent out to ambush infiltrators trying to work their way through the fence or observe our own guards on the guard posts and along the fence.

Patrolling in the DMZ is a deadly game of nerves. Although the fighting technically ended on 27 July 1953, incidents since then number in the thousands. (After the announced pullout, the number of incidents has dropped, believing by some to be an effort by the North to prove they are "good guys" to get the American forces out of Korea. The latest development to "delay action" in the face of the North's buildup may be a double-edged sword. It could force the NKs to back off, or, as some fear, may force them to a showdown as their support in China and the Soviet Union ebbs.)

The knowledge that the North is an unpredictable enemy and the number of dead since the truce numbers in the hundreds keeps the Indianhead soldiers on their toes—alert and ready. Sloppy patrolling and soldiering is answered with a quick transfer out of the company and into a dead-end job.

After we had walked through several tree-lines and along a series of rice paddies to a wooded hill, we stopped to camouflage ourselves with branches

During the day, American and ROK patrols inside the DMZ look primarily for any signs of North Korean infiltrators, such as holes in the fence, footprints, etc. They also have to be on the lookout for booby-traps and freshly planted mines. Army photo.

and foliage while the patrol leader, a young lieutenant, called the Battalion TOC. Patrol plans are often changed once inside the (DMZ) via code over the radio. "It keeps everyone on their toes," one S-3 officer explained.

After decoding the instructions from battalion, the (patrol leader) called his men around him, spread a map out on the ground, and in a half-whisper outlined the new route.

"We're going to work our way to this ridge here," he said, pointing to the map, "and check on what they've been doing on this small hill just across the MDL (Military Demarcation Line). After that we'll work our way back off this ridge and go around this hill to a creek. We'll follow the creek to this point where a dried-up creek bed runs into it. We think they are using that ravine to sneak past our boys on 116 since we can't see into it at night. After that we'll go back to the original route, finishing up the patrol along 116's hill."

He folded up the map and nodded to the crew. We moved forward carefully—we weren't sure if the North Koreans knew we were in the area and wanted to get to the first ridge and catch them working. (It is not unusual for patrols to move in the open, just to let the North know they are inside the DMZ working.) The Indianhead soldiers, well aware the North didn't want anyone spying on their activities, were extra careful and moved through the woods quietly, using hand signals only.

An hour later the lieutenant and an NCO crawled forward to take a look at the suspicious hill while the rest of the patrol formed a hasty defense near the top of the ridge. They returned a few minutes later and offered to take Jim and me forward. We quickly agreed and followed them to a well-hidden position where we could look down on the smaller hill. A small patch of cleared ground could be seen but no movement. Either they just weren't working that day or had seen us and melted into the surrounding trees. In either case they were up to something. We moved back to the patrol and sat down.

"Looks to me like an O-P or L-P," the lieutenant said, looking at Jim and me.

"Kind of close to the MDL, isn't it?" Jim asked.

"Yeah, but not unusual—they keep doing all kinds of weird things to keep us under pressure."

The first part of our mission completed, we moved off the hill toward our second objective. To keep northern eyes from seeing us, we circled a hill and crossed a small swamp, then followed the woods up and over a second hill, down into the thickly wood-lined creek. After sloshing through what was supposed to be a dry creek bed for half an hour, we reached an open area and were only a few meters from the creek bed we wanted to check.

While the rest of the patrol hid in the wood, the patrol leader, one other soldier, Jim and I moved up to the fence and MDL A well-worn path along one side of the ravine confirmed that it was being used, and on a regular basis. We made a few notes, I took some pictures, and we went back to the patrol, waiting until we were well hidden from prying eyes before sitting down to talk over what we had found. Everyone agreed the thing to do was bring in some engineers and fill the creek bed with barbed wire as close to the MDL as possible, forcing the infiltrators to cross the line where they could be seen— cutting them off.

The last of our patrol would be a sweep along the woods at the bottom of 116, then working our way up the hill in a giant "S." Again we would be looking for any signs of infiltrators trying to get close to our own positions. As we walked along the hill we had to pick our way past rolls of rusting barbed wire. On top of a small knoll we found the shattered remains of what had been a fortified defensive position during the war.

The patrol took a break and began looking around the hillside; finally the lieutenant sat down beside Jim and me.

"Way it looks to me," he said quietly, "this must have been a platoon defensive area. Part of the company holding this hill in the last days of the war. They got hit, hard. There's still a lot of brass around plus other junk, trip flares wired to trees, grenade handles and other stuff. One other thing," he looked around, "they must have thrown some pretty heavy stuff in here the way those old trees are chewed up."

Jim and I looked around. The junk of war littered the ground. When the patrol moved again, toward the guard post, the ghost of the long-dead battle cast a grim reminder over us. There had been a shooting war there. It wasn't really over, only the shooting was called off. Yet this was still a combat zone, the shooting was only the pull of a trigger away.

As we neared the guard post and walked into the open fire zone surrounding it. I felt my muscles relax. I hadn't realized how tense I had been for the past few hours.

At the guard post, as we waited for the jeeps to pick us up, Jim talked with some of the soldiers. We now shared a common ground, our first ani-

JOURNAL: 297 DAYS LEFT

The guard towers and barbed wire that ring our compound fade into the early morning fog, leaving the impression that the entire country is fringed and criss-crossed by these Korean War relics. They seem to be just waiting for the hostilities to resume, standing erect, proud that they've remained without suffering defeat or surrender since first given the task to "hold at all costs" several decades ago. They appear confident that their patience will someday pay off.

mosity having disappeared somewhere in the DMZ. On the way back, two men rode with us and Jim asked one how he felt about patrolling between the two Koreas.

"Like it ain't over yet," the soldier said thoughtfully. "The shooting has stopped, but not the war."

There was, I noticed, tension in his voice and his youthful face didn't have the glow so many young soldiers have. He never said how many patrols he had been on, or how long he had been in Korea.

A year in Korea is a nerve-wracking experience for American soldiers. There's no shooting combat—just a combat of nerves along the DMZ.

· 18 ·

Guard Post Ouellette

Death was the enemy and he hated it . . . it never intimidated him, nor did he honor it by glancing over his shoulder at it, as the rest of us do. He knew the unseen rifleman would find him, no matter where he hid, and he followed no strange roads to avoid it. It didn't matter how often it missed. There would always be a final bullet in the chamber. —Jimmy Cannon

JOURNAL: 143 DAYS LEFT

North Korea looks like desolate wasteland. Standing at the lookout post at Ouellette, I could see the gigantic flags at PanMunJom off to the left, peeking over the clouds. Looks ridiculous.

*S*ome American soldiers called it the edge of the world, others considered it the closest they ever hoped to be to a living hell—the 2nd Infantry Division compound of Guard Post Ouellette, located only a few yards south of the MDL, that meandering, unrestricted chain of wooden markers inside the DMZ that officially separates North from South Korea.

Soldiers from the 2nd Division stationed at Ouellette had one mission there; to monitor enemy border activity and alert rear combat elements just before Ouellette could be devastated by an attack from the north. A few well-placed mortar rounds is all it would take. There's little else the soldiers could do except hold the compound for as many hours, or minutes, as possible. Reinforcements or rescue would be out of the question.

During the day, the DMZ is a desolate no man's land—the most heavily armed border in the world. At night, the fence line and its string of look out posts, such as Ouellette, look like a string of pearls, hiding its deadly legacy of infiltration attempts and North Korean attacks on American and South Korean foot patrols and sentry posts. Army Photo.

There would be no chance of survival at Ouellette if the North Korean Army ever punched a hole through the DMZ on its way to attacking Seoul via the Western Corridor invasion route. Ouellette was not designed to be a fortress against attack. It was simply a very vulnerable lookout post, almost like bait tempting the rat.

One soldier, while on patrol inside the DMZ in the mid-seventies explained the pessimism that affects nearly everyone during his tour of duty at Guard Post Ouellette: "This is hell's playground. If North Korea attacks, the U.S. Army wouldn't even check to see if we have any survivors. They'd just

JOURNAL: 267 DAYS LEFT

I have been to the edge of hell. Here they call it the DMZ, and when I look into another man's eyes—he's still just a teenager—I see fear, for he is here 24-7. We know each other's questions but no one cares to state the answers, for reality is too intense. We try to block out the bad and flood our thoughts with what remains that is good. But reality is such a hard thing to ignore, and there's very little of anything good about serving so close to hell, especially when we can look across the MDL and see that hell only a few yards away.

scratch us off the list, notify our next of kin, and mobilize the country for World War III. We're merely the sacrificial lambs to get the game started."

Despite the odds-against outcome, every American soldier stationed at Ouellette was a volunteer (or so their commanding officer says, but anyone who's ever been in the Army knows the difference between volunteering and being volunteered).

They were neither suicidal nor crazy, these young American soldiers stationed at the edge of the world—they were just doing the job they'd been trained to do; as infantrymen, radar specialists, and artillery forward observers. Still, they hoped they wouldn't die doing their jobs at Ouellette, and hoped the North Koreans decide it's just too nice a day to go to war. They looked forward to that day when they could walk out from the rusty barbed-wire fence that surrounds that desolate hell-hole situated on a remote hilltop deep in the Devil's Playground.

In 2003, fifty years after the Armistice Agreement was signed at nearby PanMunJom, the mission at Guard Post Ouellette—and the patrolling of the DMZ—was turned over to the ROKs. U.S. personnel were still part of the UNC contingent at the JSA.

During the day, the sentries at Guard Post Ouellette, and other compounds along the DMZ in the 1960s and '70s relied on binoculars to monitor enemy activity. At night, they secured noisemakers such as bells and empty tin cans with rocks inside onto the perimeter fence, hoping it would alert them to enemy infiltration.

Night vision goggles and heat sensors in recent years have made it easier to detect North Korean mischief, but hasn't prevented it completely. Photo by Gary L. Bloomfield.

JOURNAL: 242 DAYS LEFT

South Korean Army soldiers with loaded machine guns were stationed at each checkpoint on highways leading to Seoul. All vehicles were being stopped at gunpoint and all identifications were checked. Trunks opened and searched. Korean police warns us to avoid driving during daylight hours in an Army jeep because North Korean guerrillas are hiding out in the surrounding hills somewhere north of Seoul. One was captured earlier and revealed the location. They're suspected to have grenade launchers and machine-guns. They've already killed two South Korean soldiers. U.S. vehicles are a favorite target for Joe Chink and his band of merry mischief makers.

Decided to turn around and just stay on the compound today.

We have been drilled not to draw attention to ourselves, especially up on the Z. This reminds me of one of those little-known Abstract Rules of Combat—"Try not to act like John Wayne, promenading up and down the lines, because if the enemy is low on ammunition, they will save every shot just for you."

"The missions will be turned over as part of a reorganization of U.S. forces in South Korea, including returning smaller bases to the South Korean government," wrote Jeremy Kirk, in *Pacific Stars and Stripes*, on April 13, 2004. "It marks U.S. forces' gradual pullback from the DMZ, a move partly inspired by high-tech, long-range weapons that make distance less important during a fight. It's also a nod to the South Korean military's increased ability."

JOURNAL: 173 DAYS LEFT

Galen Geer and I, along with one of the Korean soldiers we work with, drove up to Guard Post Ouellette, which is situated just yards south of the Military Demarcation Line. Our Korean translator had been jabbering all during the two-hour drive from Camp Casey until we got to the Southern Barrier Fence of the DMZ. Then he saw the barbed wire, the minefields, the lookout towers, and the apprehension in the faces of the American and ROK soldiers stationed there, and suddenly he fell quiet, barely saying anything during the three hours we were inside the Z.

I think it just dawned on him that the North Koreans probably don't think too kindly of our allies, and might make his short life painfully miserable if he were captured while we're there. The following article was written a few months after Galen left Korea, published in *Soldier of Fortune* magazine. And it was written before the 2nd Infantry Division relinquished the DMZ mission to ROK Army forces more than twenty years later.

THE FENCE

By Galen Geer, for Soldier of Fortune *magazine, December 1979*

Summer or winter, a night of guard duty along Korea's DMZ is a nerve-wracking experience. While fighting off swarms of bugs in summer and penetrating cold in winter, the men of the 2nd Infantry Division stand guard along the last combat line of the U.S. Army—the Korean DMZ.

The fence is more of a psychological barrier than actual obstruction to the north. It is a storm-fence topped with multiple strands of concertina. Spotlights line the fence and bunkers spaced along its length are manned by ROK soldiers, except for the 300-meter section bordering the road to PanMunJom. Its only real function is to stop infiltrators. Along its entire length is a strip of soft sand, kept neatly raked by patrolling soldiers. Should any infiltrators cross the boundary their crossing would be visible by the disturbed sand.

The soldiers who pull DMZ duty are confident nothing will happen during their tour on the fence. They are, however, fatalistic about their chances for survival should a new shooting war start.

"We're dead, that's all there is to it. We don't have enough ammo to fire up a small patrol. All we can do is yell 'bang' and let the world know they're coming."

That is the job of the American soldiers along the fence. Equipped with a PRC-77 radio, flares and a dozen rounds of small arms ammunition, they wait and watch.

"I've tried to write my wife about the fence," one friendly sergeant said, "but what do I say? 'Sweetheart, this is where I'll die if these crazy people ever start shooting again?'"

Each man who pulls duty on the fence learns to deal with it in his own way. A few can't and request transfers, although most believe it is the only time in their Army careers they are soldiers being soldiers and not soldiers playing boy scouts.

During the day fence duty is little more than traffic cop work; checking passes, raising and lowering the guardrail across the road. At night, however, the fence and the duty change dramatically. After dark the DMZ is a free-fire zone. Meaning anything that moves can be shot. Ambush patrols which go into the no man's land at night are free to open fire on targets and frequently do.

The fence itself is schizophrenic. During the day, nothing but rusting steel and wire, at night lights transform it into a snakelike creature glowing across distant hills. To soldiers looking into the pitch black beyond the lights, it is a thin wall separating them from the unseen enemy.

Every night patrols move through the gate after a short meeting between the patrol leader and the NCO on the fence. An exact count is made of the men going into the DMZ and locations where the patrol will be during the night. Every soldier on the fence knows where the patrol is supposed to be and at what time. As the night drags on, the war of nerves begins.

A bush crackling in the dark brings everyone back from his half-sleep to begin the long wait to find out who or what is on the other side of the fence. Sometimes, too often for some men, a distinctly human sound is heard and all talking stops. The only question in everyone's mind becomes, "Who is it? Ours or theirs?"

Loaded magazines are tapped in M-16s and the sergeant explains the patrol is not supposed to be there. Along the fence the half-dozen American soldiers wait, knowing all they would be able to do is give an alarm before they died. After nearly an hour without another sound, the men begin to

Soldiers patrolling the southern half of the DMZ are on constant alert for enemy activity. North Korean soldiers have ambushed foot patrols and passing military vehicles well south of the Military Demarcation Line—that string of simple fence posts marking the actual border between North and South Korea. Photo by Gary L. Bloomfield.

relax. "They" would have done something—thrown a rock, shouted, anything to shatter nerves.

The hours pass slowly after any incident along the fence. When the patrol returns and is counted back through the gate—one man at a time to be sure everyone is there and there are no hitch-hikers—the sergeant asks where they were, accusing them of being lost.

"We weren't lost," the patrol leader explains. "We double-checked our position so we could watch that old bridge."

I asked a patrol member once what kind of night it was.

"Routine," he answered, then stretched out to sleep, ignoring the bouncing truck.

"Routine," flashed in my mind. Routine to the 2nd Infantry Division soldier along Korea's DMZ is a 300-meter frontline, where no shots are fired and nerves are shattered.

JOURNAL

My father was stationed in Japan when North Korea invaded the south. While combat units stateside were mobilized, those troops in Japan were rushed into the fray. My dad was one of them. He also served two tours in Vietnam.

He didn't talk much about Korea but showed me some graphically brutal photos of enemy atrocities . . . the bodies of hundreds of American soldiers, their hands bound behind their back.

When I was growing up, my dad never let me play with guns, saying war is not something to pretend play. In November 1990, I wrote the following article, for *VFW* magazine, as a tribute to all veterans, but mostly for my father, Army Command Sergeant Major Robert D. Bloomfield.

GRANDPA WAS A HERO

Every afternoon when I get home from work I can always count on Bobby waving to me from across the street. Sometimes he's playing war with the neighborhood boys, but he'll always pop out from behind a bush or a tree and say "Hi" before ducking back down to hide from the "bad guys."

And sometimes he's sitting on the porch with his grandfather, who lives next door to Bobby and his family. That old war horse sure must have some

"He took me to the wall and there was a statue of a soldier and his son, so I asked Grandpa if that was him and my dad. He just smiled." Photo of the War Memorial in Eldora, Colorado, by Liam H. Flake.

interesting stories to tell because more than once I've seen Bobby sitting at his feet for an hour or two, listening closely to his grandfather's tales.

But one day I came home and Bobby was sitting alone by the curb. I waved, but he just ignored me, so I walked over and sat down next to him.

"Having a rough day, Squirt?" I joked, jabbing him in the arm.

Usually, whenever I call him that, Bobby starts to pick a fight, but this time he just nodded his head, and continued to mope.

"I've been wondering something. I've seen you and your grandfather sittin' over there on the porch quite a bit. I'll bet he's got some really neat stories. You wanna share a few of 'em with me?"

Bobby didn't say a word, so we just sat there for a few minutes. Then suddenly he got this big smile and started talking like a whirlwind . . .

"My grandpa was in a war," Bobby boasted. "He called it Korrie or something like that."

"Do you mean Korea?" I asked.

"That's it! I'm not sure when it was, but he says my mom was just a little girl, so it musta been a hundred years ago cause I think she's pretty old!" Then he looked around to see if she heard that. When he was sure it was safe, we both laughed.

"I don't know where my grandpa was, but he said it's at least ten times farther than travellin' to my Uncle Joe's house, so it's gotta be somewheres on the other side of the universe!

"He said it took ten days just to cross the ocean. I could probably walk there faster than that ship. Heck, I could get there in two seconds if I had a Mach One Star Cruiser! Grandpa don't even know what that is. I took him to see the movie once, but he fell asleep!" Then Bobby took a deep breath, collected his thoughts, and revved up his motor again.

"Grandpa don't even knows what a laser blaster is either! He showed me a picture of him with this prehistoric rifle! Said one time he shot two Chi-Coms in five seconds. I don't know what a ChiCom is, but I told him that with a laser blaster I could evaporate a whole country with one mega-burst!"

Bobby hopped to his feet and started "evaporating" every house in the neighborhood (except his and mine) with his finger. Just as quickly he plopped down again and started pouting, ripping out clumps of dirt and grass.

"He went back there a few years ago, to Ko-re-a. Said he didn't rec-ognize it. Everything was new and everybody he met gave him flowers and thanked him and they called him a hero. He showed me pictures."

I remembered one day the old man met me at the mail boxes and showed me those photos. Couldn't remember where most of them were shot but he could name every GI in each photo.

Bobby's grandfather one time took him to the wall in town and he cried when he saw his best friend's name there. Bobby hoped someday he too could get his name on a wall. Photo of the War Memorial in Eldora, Colorado, by Liam H. Flake.

"One time he took me to the wall across town and showed me the names of his buddies who died over there, including his best friend. Said he still thinks about him all these years, and hopes to see him again soon, but I don't know what he means by that."

I started to explain it but figured that was something his mom or dad could do better.

"Maybe someday I can get my name on a wall."

I wanted to say "No you don't" but he's too young to know why.

"And there was a statue of a soldier with his son, so I asked Grandpa if that was him and my dad."

"What did he say?"

"Nothing, he just smiled."

"Grandpa always fusses when I plays space warriors or combat, or even cowboys and Indians with my friends. He comes limping out of the house, waving his cane, saying we shouldn't make a game of killing no one. My friends just laughs and runs off to somewheres else. I takes Grandpa inside and we plays checkers. He says war is a lot like checkers, but I sure don't know what's the same about them."

I started to explain the similarities, but just then Bobby started crying, fighting to hold back the tears.

"Grandpa says men don't cry, but I guess it don't matter now what he says."

I wanted to ask Bobby what was wrong, but I knew eventually he'd get around to it. We sat there a while before Bobby finally opened up.

"Grandpa died a few days ago," he whispered.

I just sat there in disbelief. I had seen quite a few cars coming and going at Bobby's house the past two days, but didn't see anything out of the ordinary, except that Bobby hadn't been outside all weekend. No wonder he was so upset.

"The funeral was this morning. Grandpa had on his uniform with all the colored ribbons. He even wore one that I gave him for being the 'World's Greatest Granddad.' Six soldiers carried his coffin, and some others fired their rifles, and another played a horn, and mom got the folded flag. After the funeral everybody came over and said Grandpa had a funeral fit for a war hero.

"I already knew Grandpa was a hero. I'm not sure what he done in the war, but I know he was a hero."

It's been a while since Bobby said goodbye to his grandfather. That feisty old warrior isn't around anymore to tell his tales, but I have a feeling his memory is going to linger for a long, long time. Hopefully Bobby won't ever be a war hero like his grandpa, but something tells me he's going to grow up and try to be just as terrific.

JOURNAL

Bobby lived across the street and every day when I got home from work, he wanted to toss a football, shoot hoops, or play catch with a baseball . . . except for the week after his grandfather died. I couldn't help but think of my own father, who died way too young and missed out on seeing our daughter—his only grandchild—grow up to be an amazing mom herself. He would be proud.

• 19 •

Lifeline to Seoul

If ever there was an ideal place for mines, it was Inchon. —Vice Admiral Arthur D. Struble, 1950

When an advancing enemy crosses water do not meet him at the water's edge. It is advantageous to allow half his force to cross and then strike. —Sun Tzu, *The Art of War*

𝒯he chain of concertina wire seems to run forever as it crests the horizon and trails far beyond. Free passage is allowed on the east side of the wire, but trespassing across means walking through a deadly minefield that's constructed to be impenetrable. Survivors of the minefield would still have to contend with trigger-happy, shoot-to-kill sentries that patrol along the fence.

Concrete bunkers with twenty-four-hour guards armed with machine-guns, and spotlights, trip flares, and other sensing devices concealed everywhere add to the invasion proof barrier against a North Korean attack.

This isn't the Demilitarized Zone thirty miles north of Seoul, or a major military command headquarters in a fortified underground bunker. It's Inchon, the vital South Korean western seaport that serves as a lifeline to the capital city of Seoul.

During the Korean War, when Communist forces invaded the south and pushed South Korean and American forces all the way to the Pusan perimeter far to the southeast, an amphibious force snuck around the peninsula and came ashore at Inchon in late September 1950. Soon Seoul was retaken and the initiative swung in favor of the UN forces, though it would take nearly three more years for both sides to agree to a ceasefire. The vulnerability of Inchon as a lifeline to Seoul has never been forgotten, especially as North Korean infiltration attempts increased in the 1970s.

PROBING THE GAUNTLET

In addition to the highly visible deterrents—the wire, the guards, and the bunkers—Inchon's overlapping defensive system reaches far beyond the shoreline. Anti-invasion devices, resembling gigantic daggers, and designed to rip gaping holes in an interloper's hull, lay submerged just below the surface waters along the shoreline. At low tide these devices are easily seen, securely anchored, and menacingly sharp, pointing seaward among moored fishing boats. But once the sea rolls back in, those daggers are concealed, unforgiving sentries.

During the hours of darkness, citizens of Inchon stay clear of the coastal area—ROK Army guards are instructed to shoot anyone suspicious who moves near the Sea Wall. It's definitely not a place for romantic interludes.

But are all these invasion precautions really necessary?

Further out on the waters, beyond the horizon, high-speed South Korean naval patrol boats with sophisticated radar and sonar equipment keep a lookout for, and are often tested by enemy infiltrators attempting to penetrate the coastline with everything from submarines and rubber dinghies, to disguised fishing boats and heavily armed warships.

Local South Korean newspapers frequently reveal these many enemy incursions: "Two North Korean spy boats fired on a South Korean government ship," reported the *Korea Herald*. Other mentions include:

"An armed North Korean spy boat was intercepted and sunk by ROK naval elements while attempting to infiltrate close to the nation's coast."

"Eight armed North Korean agents were captured when a Communist spy boat was sunk while approaching the coast of South Korea."

Many of these enemy probes occur in the dark of night, and even though a majority are intercepted, it is also unknown how many more succeed in landing North Korean commandos on the southern mainland, some to strike quickly, strike hard and head back to safety; others to blend in with the local populous, maybe make it to Seoul and blend in with the masses, and lay low until a designated time and place to launch and fulfill their mission.

HOLD AT ALL COSTS

The importance of defending Inchon was best explained by a ROK Army commander when asked to justify the overlapping defensive systems that surround the port city.

"Losing Inchon would be like slitting Korea's throat. Without the necessary supplies delivered by foreign transport ships, Seoul would be completely cut

*The Korean War Memorial at Inchon com-
memorates the U.S. Marine landing in late September 1950. Pacific Stars and Stripes.*

off. An enemy invasion at Inchon, while attacking north to Seoul, would be a
secondary battle front. The enemy's primary avenue of attack would be across the
DMZ. This maneuver, if aided by enough men and firepower could surround
Seoul, which then could only last a few weeks before it would be captured."

Former U.S. Secretary of Defense Harold Brown added that "South
Korea would have to divert forces from their primary mission of repelling an
attack on the DMZ to counter special warfare activities of the north" such
as an amphibious landing at Inchon. "The defense of Inchon is, in essence,"
stressed a ROK Army commander, "the defense of all of Korea."

• 20 •

The Tunnels

All wars are deception. —Sun Tzu

Those expert at preparing defenses consider it fundamental to rely on the strengths of such obstacles as mountains, rivers and foothills. They make it impossible for the enemy to know where to attack. They conceal themselves as under the nine-layered ground. —Tu Yu

 $\mathcal{A}$ cross the peace table at PanMunJom, via the hotline that links Seoul to Pyongyang (which sometimes remains disconnected for years), continuously broadcast on radio and TV, and printed daily in Communist newspapers, the North Korean regime has continuously shown the world its mission of "peaceful" reunification of a divided Korea.

But while the negotiations opened once-barricaded doors between north and south for a long-dreamed of exchange of political prisoners, and homeland visits for separated families, the Demilitarized Zone was being turned into a maze of underground invasion tunnels by Communist engineers and laborers.

THE VORACIOUS TUNNEL RATS

Soon after the American pullout of Vietnam, Kim Il Sung solicited China's approval to attack the south. While outwardly espousing peace and a cooperative reunification, Kim ordered the surreptitious construction of tunnels under the DMZ. These would be used by infiltrators to sneak under the minefields and barbed wire fortifications of the southern zone, coming out behind allied lines.

In mid-November 1974, a ROK Army squad of soldiers was patrolling inside the DMZ when they noticed steam rising from the ground. At first they thought it might be a hot spring, but while looking around, they came under machine-gun fire from a North Korean guard post across the MDL.

Five days later, when a UNC inspection team revisited the site and uncovered the tunnel, an explosive device detonated, killing a U.S. Navy senior

ROK Army soldiers use mine detectors to check a North Korean invasion tunnel for booby traps. When the first tunnel was discovered, an American officer and ROK officer were killed when an undetected explosive was detonated. Korean Overseas Information Service photo.

officer and a ROK Marine major. Five American servicemen and one ROK soldier were also injured in the blast. Once the area was secured, and no more booby traps were hidden, the excavation team found that the tunnel extended one thousand meters south of the MDL. It was reinforced with concrete pillars and slabs, and had lights and electric power.

"The discovery of an invasion tunnel dug by the North Koreans under the Demilitarized Zone was proof enough that the basic policy toward this Republic has not changed at all in spite of all the peace rhetoric Pyongyang has vended all these years," reported the *Korea Herald* in 1978.

"Discovery of the PanMunJom tunnel was a combination of luck and persistence. Its general location was first reported by a North Korean defector. His information was confirmed by such seismic and physical signs as underground explosions, oddly colored vegetation and suspicious pools of water," wrote James Wallace for *U.S. News & World Report*, November 6, 1978. "But more than 100 boreholes drilled by American and South Korean tunnel-neutralization teams over 18 months failed to locate anything. Finally North Korean engineers gave the game away."

"On the morning of June 10, 1978, only two weeks before the Korean War anniversary, a powerful underground noise shattered the tranquility of Korea's Demilitarized Zone," reported the Korean Overseas Information Service. "The blast from underground occurred about 400 meters south of the Military Demarcation Line that divides Korea into north and south. Its power sent to the air a plastic casing lining which had been inserted into a three-inch borehole which had been drilled into the ground in 1975. Soon, water spewed forth 12 meters high from underground. Investigations by the United Nations Command revealed that the blast was touched off by a team of North Korean workers burrowing beneath the Demilitarized Zone. They had inadvertently intersected the bore holes which had been drilled just for such purposes."

Initially the North Korean delegates at PanMunJom denied any knowledge of the tunnels, saying it was the Americans and South Koreans who were trying to tunnel under the DMZ to invade the North. Then, with mounting evidence, the North tried to say the tunnels were actually coal mines, even though there was no coal in the area. But to prove their point, they painted the walls black to resemble anthracite.

Despite the discoveries and setbacks, the north has not abandoned its tunneling. Underground explosions continued to rock the DMZ and it was a constant effort for UN forces to detect and uncover the work. Discovery of the third invasion tunnel came from an unlikely source.

"First hints of this particular tunnel began to surface in September 1975 when a North Korean engineer named Kim Pu Song fled south," reported the Korean Overseas Information Service, in October 1978. "Kim

supplied the vital intelligence that he had himself engaged in tunnel survey-
ing and designing operations in that area since 1972. Kim's information had
led the United Nations Command to bore a large number of holes in 1975
below the southern portion of the zone. A huge drilling machine had been
set up. Thus, when one of the bore holes erupted at 6:15 a.m. inside the
United Nations Command territory on June 10, the defector's intelligence
had been confirmed."

DISCOVERED BUT UNDETERRED

In another article in the *Korea Herald*, Ahn Byung Joon wrote, "It is very
clear that Kim Il Sung never abandoned his intention to invade South Korea
while advocating 'peaceful unification of Korea' in words. By approving these
underground tunnels, [Kim] may have wanted either to infiltrate a contingent
of guerrilla forces or to carry out a surprise attack on Seoul."

Exactly when that "surprise attack on Seoul" might occur was revealed
by the defector Kim Pu Song, who was told "that the tunnels were meant
to send troops and weapons for a surprise attack against the south when the
'decisive' moment was announced. That moment, he said, was understood to
be October 10, 1975, the 30th anniversary of the party's founding."

The discovery of the tunnels may have hindered that "decisive moment" but it has not curtailed the tunneling efforts. "Kim Pu Song said that
he had worked as surveyor-designer on the tunnel just discovered, and had
witnessed at least eight others being dug; one in Kaesung, two in the Kor-
agpo area, two between Korangpo and Pyongyang, and three in the middle
eastern front sector."

That threat is very real to allied observers of North Korean strategy.
Upon completion—with ventilation and lights, high enough for a soldier to
walk upright and wide enough for transport vehicles—each tunnel could ac-
commodate thousands of troops an hour. If done at night and with minimal
noise, an invasion force that size could easily break through allied-controlled
lines and wipe-out frontline units trapped with nowhere to escape.

Hundreds of guerrillas annually infiltrate the south—swimming to shore
in the dark of night, hopping a plane to Japan then back to South Korea,
or simply walking across the MDL are but three of the many ways Communist guerrillas probe the peninsula, all without the help of tunnels. Still,
some observers feel that the North Korean communists will use the tunnels
as a potential pipeline to supply military equipment to insurgents operating
in the south.

CUTTING OFF ANY ESCAPE TO THE SOUTH

But the time and effort expended, plus the complexity of each tunnel reveals that more than just a supply pipeline or an avenue for a few hundred North Korean infiltrators were intended for these subterranean corridors to the south. "According to Ministry of National Defense officials, the second discovered tunnel is wide enough for the passage of 30,000 North Korean troops per hour," wrote *Korea Herald* reporter Kang Sang Yun in October 1978. "Considering that the tunnel is only four kilometers north of Freedom Bridge, it is assumed that the North Korean Communists have plotted to occupy the Imjin River area and the main invasion route as quickly as possible in preparation for a surprise attack on South Korea."

"Buried beneath 73 meters of solid granite, this tunnel was designed to withstand aerial bombings and thus provide for the rapid movement of troops and weapons for a surprise assault on allied posts just above the Imjin River," reported the ROK government in its pamphlet, *Tunnels of War: North Korea Catacombs the DMZ.*

This tactic, coming up behind forward-based units of the ROK Army and U.S. 2nd Division along the DMZ would trap the allied forces north of the Imjin. Thousands of American and South Korean soldiers would thus be caught in this deadly vise. And by annihilating the south's vital first line of defense, the Communist attack would meet little resistance until it reached the outskirts of Seoul. Obviously, South Korean forces would be immediately alerted to cut off the invasion route, plus U.S. Air Force planes would be scrambled and exact a heavy toll during the onslaught, but it would still be a very deadly affair. (Second Infantry Division forces have since been relocated further south of the DMZ but within hours of an invasion, they would be rushed to the front to block the main invasion routes to Seoul.)

"Even a relatively small force of 2,000 armed enemy troops, probably uniformed as South Koreans, could create havoc," continued James Wallace for *U.S. News & World Report.* "An authority explains: 'They could shoot up rear areas, create confusion and spread doubts about whether the guy down the road was on the wrong side. An enemy platoon with rocket launchers might keep an entire battalion at bay for hours.' No single tunnel could create that much disorder. But no authority in South Korea knows how many more underground corridors exist, including remote eastern regions of the border region. Officials suspect that at least a dozen more tunnels are under construction. Others may already be completed except for final exits, which would be opened only as an invasion starts."

"If North Korean infiltrators were dressed in South Korean uniforms, and also attacked U.S. forces near the DMZ, that would have a devastating effect on the trust between the U.S. troops and their South Korean allies," said David Maxwell, retired Army special forces colonel, and an analyst at Georgetown University's Center for Security Studies in Washington. (He was interviewed for Voice of America in mid-August 2014.)

"It has now been established that the zone is not only pockmarked by these horrendous weapons; it is also catacombed by an unknown number of secret underground tunnels dug by North Korea to infiltrate men and weapons to the south," published by the Korean Overseas Information Service, in October 1978. "Evidently, they were built with the intention of mounting a surprise attack on the Republic of Korea."

A tunnel capable of handling thirty thousand troops an hour seems hard to imagine, but when the first tunnel was discovered on November 15, 1974, it was 1.2 meters high and one meter wide. The second tunnel, detected four months later measured two meters high and 2.2 meters wide. The third tunnel has similar dimensions. Also, each tunnel is fortified with steel beams and arcs, lighting, ventilation, and railroad tracks to transport vehicles and heavy artillery pieces.

"The third tunnel is about twice as big as the first one in scale, sufficient for the passage of combat troops carrying heavy firearms in three to four columns," revealed a *Korea Herald* editorial.

"Its location, 44 kilometers from Seoul, the closest of the three tunnels so far found, at the threshold of the Munsan (the first major village just south of the Imjin River) to Seoul route, indicates that it was designed for a direct and immediate swoop at the capital city."

ATTACK SCENARIO

The Senate's Committee on Armed Services report in 1979 revealed the most likely invasion scenario:

"In an attack upon the south, North Korea would have the advantage of choosing the time and place. It could concentrate its already great firepower advantage and attack South Korea giving little or no warning. South Korea has 24 company-size and one battalion-size strongpoints along the DMZ. However, there are many weak spots along the DMZ, and it will be difficult to stop North Korea there. Tunnels first discovered in 1974 could also be used to gain surprise behind the DMZ. The ample North Korean river-crossing equipment provides another option for invading South Korea.

"Military analysts believe that a North Korean attack would probably use the Kaesong-Munsan-Seoul corridor with secondary attacks through the

Chorwan Valley and diversionary attacks to the east. The North Korean attack would place heavy reliance upon the shock effect and firepower of its nearly 2,000 tanks. The results of an attack upon Seoul via these corridors would probably be determined by the ability of ROK forces to hold the heavily fortified FEBA-ALPHA line two to five miles south of the DMZ. Substantial improvements are required and major efforts are underway to improve this line."

WARNING TIME

"Warning time is the single most critical factor in the military equation," the Armed Services Committee report continued. "Warning of a pending attack can be either strategic or tactical. Strategic warning is based on broad political and military indicators while tactical warning is provided by precise evidence that an actual attack is imminent.

"North Korea is a totally closed society thus reducing the possibility of tactical warning. In addition, since North Korean forces are currently in position to attack the south, strategic warning due to large troop movements may not be forthcoming. The impact of U.S. troop withdrawal on U.S./ROK ability to detect a potential surprise attack is unclear. The problem of warning time is so critical that whether a withdrawal proceeds safely may be subject to an adequate resolution of this problem."

SUMMARY OF THE BALANCE

"In summary, North Korean military capabilities currently give it significant advantages in the critical first days of fighting, if the north can achieve tactical and strategic surprise. These North Korean advantages are at least partly offset by the presence of the U.S. 2nd Infantry Division and its supporting forces. If the war continued, the balance should shift to the south as it mobilized its reserve forces and as U.S. assistance began to arrive on the peninsula.

SPENDING FOOL'S GOLD

Pyongyang's all-out preparation for war has decimated its economy. "It is believed that North Korea funneled a huge sum of money and manpower into the building of the third invasion tunnel, which was described as a difficult job," cites South Korean Ministry experts. "These activities are considered even more sinister and unthinkable in view of the fact that their economy has virtually gone broke to finance each one."

"They're tunneling like crazy under the DMZ," stated U.S. Representative Lester Wolff, former chairman of the House Asian Affairs Subcommittee. "They're also building a vast network of corridors into the south. In the north they're putting whole industrial plants and a lot of civilian facilities underground. Everything's gone underground in North Korea. It's a very ominous sign."

But according to former "beloved comrade leader" Kim Il Sung, no sacrifice is too great if the end result is the reunification of Korea—even if that goal can only be achieved by force. "Kim declared that once a new war erupted in Korea, he would have nothing but the truce line to lose, but a whole Korea to gain," added the ROK government in the pamphlet *Tunnels of War*. But, South Korea warns, when that Communist force is unleashed it will be met by an equally devastating allied counterattack.

In anticipation of retaliatory strikes by UN and South Korean forces soon after an invasion, the Pyongyang regime has devoted up to 30 percent of its gross national product on not just the building of tunnels in the DMZ but also entire underground cities scattered throughout North Korea, most of which are undetected by satellite reconnaissance.

"I WANT WHAT BIG BROTHER CHINA'S GOT"

How complex these tunnels and underground facilities are is not publicly known in the West, but they're probably patterned after China's vast subterranean network. Easily within range of Soviet missiles and air bases, China's major cities are capable of surviving a devastating bombardment without overwhelming loss of life among its key leaders or crucial industry . . . and all because of the tunnels and below-ground facilities.

The Viet Cong owed much of their success to the network of tunnels in Vietnam (which perplexed American patrols in hot pursuit, only to stall when the VC "disappeared" without any trace). In fact North Korea was more than just an observer of how the Viet Cong used tunnels to their advantage.

"North Korea is the world's most-tunneled nation. North Korea's expertise in digging tunnels for warfare was demonstrated during the Vietnam War. North Korea sent about 100 tunnel warfare experts to Vietnam to help dig the 250 km tunnels for the North Vietnamese and Viet Cong troops in South Vietnam. The tunnels were instrumental in the Vietnamese victory," noted Han Ho Suk, director of the Center for Korean Affairs, on April 24, 2003.

At the same time North Korea was creating a catacomb of tunnels under the DMZ, they were upgrading and expanding their military. In fact during the seventies North Korea was considered to be greater than the combined armament of the 2nd Division, UN and South Korean forces, as revealed in a report to the U.S. Senate's Committee on Armed Services, dated January 23, 1979. The report stated:

"Since the Spring of 1978, a fundamental reassessment of North Korean military capabilities, conducted jointly by the Central Intelligence Agency, Defense Intelligence Agency, Army Intelligence and Security Command, and other U.S. intelligence organizations, has been underway. The reassessment postulates a substantially larger and more offensively oriented North Korean military posture than heretofore assumed.

"More specifically, the new threat assessment credits the North Korean Army with 560–600,000 men instead of 440,000, and 40 divisions (including separate brigades) rather than 29, with a significantly larger and more formidable array of armor and artillery, including comparatively modern Soviet-designed main battle tanks, rocket launchers, large-caliber tube artillery and air defense systems."

More recent assessments show an overwhelming number of combat troops, tanks, artillery pieces, rockets and missiles, warships, and fighter jets and bombers. But underlying those numbers is the simple fact that many are vintage models from the 1960s and '70s, even outdated armaments that would serve as nothing but target practice for the superior weaponry of the American and South Korean military alliance.

Three other important factors, which adversely affect North Korean military readiness, are the lack of training hours on the weapons systems they'd go to war with, the shortage of fuel to power those ships, planes, and vehicles, and the severe lack of spare parts to keep everything functioning at a combat level.

Bottom line? Similar to the bluster Saddam Hussein boasted about his military, when coalition forces were prepping to liberate Kuwait and invade Iraq during Desert Storm, Pyongyang also displays a superiority attitude to mask an inferiority complex. Any attempt by North Korea to invade the south, might initially cause chaos in the south, especially in Seoul which is vulnerable to a rocket barrage, but within days the might and muscle of the United States and South Korea would bare its teeth and destroy everything north of the 38th Parallel.

The network of tunnels and shelters under North Korea and the DMZ merely gives the Pyongyang regime a means to extend their country's lifespan while bankrupting their economy . . . but it doesn't prevent the inevitable total destruction of North Korea.

JOURNAL

There's always an eeriness about Guard Post Ouellette. No movement or sound nearby. Not even any birds. But off in the distance is a low rumble, like thunder. They say it's North Korean artillery just letting the Manchus know they're prepped and ready for a fight.

Now I'm learning about the tunnels and how they fire those big guns to mask any noise from underground explosions as they advance further south under the DMZ.

"For weaker sides in conflicts, the best defense traditionally has been the earth," retired Army Special Forces Colonel David Maxwell said. "It provides cover, and the deeper you go, the harder it is for enemy bombs to penetrate." In addition to the tunnels under the DMZ, the North Koreans have built massive underground caverns and warehouses, with the capability to squirrel away every piece of military hardware in their inventory. Their subterranean network includes barracks, hospitals, even industrial complexes to survive any bombing campaign intent on destroying the regime and decimate its war machine. But cowering underground only prolongs the inevitable, because eventually those North Korean tanks and artillery guns, rockets, and missiles and fighter aircraft have to come out from hiding, and that's when the superiority of the U.S. and South Korean arsenals will lay waste to anything and everything with hostile intent.

JOURNAL

Mid-2018: Recent meetings between the U.S. and North Korea lead politicians and diplomats in D.C., Seoul, Tokyo, Beijing, and Moscow, and news reporters around the world to believe that after more than sixty years, there will finally be lasting peace on the Korean Peninsula, and that steps are being taken to denuclearize the communist north. United Nations inspectors will be allowed in to verify the dismantling and destruction of nuclear warheads and components. Test sites have and will be destroyed and, to remove the temptation of reprocessing spent fuel rods, nuclear power plants (which have never actually provided any power to any residents or factories in the area) will be replaced by hydroelectric plants that will eventually provide electricity to the entire country, and with that power, industrialization will finally bring the masses into the nineteenth century. (The Potemkin Village of Pyongyang attempts to be a twentieth-century metropolis to outsiders, while the privileged elite pretend not to notice that underneath it all, the infrastructure is perilously close to collapse. Certainly outside of the capital city, the rest of the country is left to rot.) In a few years' time the country will be declared nuclear free, and the whole world will rejoice, and Pyongyang will quietly smirk and allow everyone to believe just that. But nothing could be further from the truth.

The possession of nuclear weapons gives North Korea legitimacy . . . at least that's what they want to believe . . . and ever since they got those damnable nukes, they've been acting like the bully on the block. Their "neighborhood" just happens to be northeast Asia where three of the most powerful economies in the world are now within striking distance. And now, even the U.S. is within range of their ICBMs. They are not simply going to give up their new toys—those nukes.

North Korea's mountainous terrain is prime real estate for massive underground caverns, entire industrial complexes, and all of it connected by a maze of tunnels. Warehouses deep inside the mountains are large enough to house fighter aircraft, tanks, missile systems and artillery pieces, barracks and support facilities for hundreds of thousands of troops . . . and nuclear warheads. (The tunnels under the DMZ are only the tip of the iceberg known by outside sources. Years ago a defector informed South Korean and U.S. forces that up to twenty invasion tunnels are in various stages of completion under the DMZ, and yet they still can't be found.)

With a purge in the top military leadership in North Korea (due to questionable loyalty to Kim Jong Un) and the paranoid secrecy infecting the Pyongyang elites, it is highly probable that there is no one person or even agency that knows or has a record of exactly where every nuclear warhead, component, delivery system and even canisters of plutonium and uranium are stored or hidden. As such, if and when UN inspectors are allowed in the country, they will be shown whatever they wish to see. They may even be allowed access to facilities no one ever heard of, including those that haven't been detected by satellites or overflight spy planes. But what they will not be granted is total access, though the North Korean leadership will insist they have been completely honest and forthright.

The common term being bantered about is "trust but verify." Trusting the North Korean leadership, after decades of deceit and blatant stretchings of the truth, is only for fools who fail to study an endless stream of promises made and promises either ignored, or broken.

And verify is an elusive goal, without any guarantee of absolute certainty. In fact, with absolute certainty I know North Korea will not give up all of its nukes, because, in their eyes, those nukes give them legitimacy and allow them to play in the sandbox with the big boys. Without nukes, they're just a wannabe third-rate country on the verge of total collapse. Those nukes are the only bargaining chips they have for much-needed aid, in the form of food, fuel, medicine, and even cash.

And just so no one mistakes the generosity of the United States, we have given millions of dollars in all of the above to ease the suffering of the masses. But along the way, everything is diverted and doled out to the privileged loyalists living in Pyongyang. We have demanded that our own inspectors accompany the food and medicine to ensure that the most needy receive it, but they are blocked at the border, reassuring our inspectors that the aid will be distributed equitable . . . to the military and the elites in Pyongyang, that is. By continuing to send any form of aid to North Korea, all we're doing is enabling the military to grow stronger and the loyalists in Pyongyang to enjoy what comforts they feel are owed to them. None but a small token of aid is given to those who need it most, and that token is only to show they are acting in good faith.

And that aid? The propaganda machine lets the masses know that it is nothing but reparations for the "wrongs" committed by the United States during the Korean War. It is also "protection" because we so fear the military might of North Korea and by appeasing them, we ensure our own safety. One of the benefits of a closed society is that the masses can be easily duped to believe anything they've been told.

(Currently sanctions are putting the squeeze on North Korea, and they will only be lessened when they act in good faith to denuclearize, which is why they're willing to play the game, but they'll play it according to their rules, which is to say whatever is needed and do whatever is needed to get the sanctions lifted, but under no circumstances will they relinquish all of their nukes, which is easy to do because no one—inside or outside of North Korea—knows exactly how many they have, or where they are, and even as UN inspectors are walking in the front door of a nuclear weapons plant or storage facility, the really potent stuff is being wheeled out the backdoor, or stashed behind an undetected false wall or under a trap door. It's the ultimate shell game, and they know how to play it better than anyone.)

Again, there is absolutely no surefire way to verify that every nuclear weapon in North Korea, and every trace of the components and elements needed to make future weapons will be dismantled, destroyed, or dispatched out of the country. They will certainly scream from the mountaintops that they have cooperated with all of our demands, but five years from now, maybe ten, when some international incident threatens to shatter the uncertain peace on the Korean Peninsula, they will again roll out the toys they supposedly no longer possessed and threaten the region with those damnable nukes they've kept hidden all this time. That is a certainty.

• *21* •

Shell-Shocked

There can be no double standard. We cannot have peace among men whose hearts find delight in killing any living creature. —Rachel Carson

It does not do to leave a live dragon out of your calculations, if you live near him. —J. R. R. Tolkien

If the enemy is within range, just remember that so are you! —Abstract Rules of Combat

They're called drainage ditches, but the man-made furrows that run parallel to every major road at the base camp of the 2nd Infantry Division was approximately three feet deep, enough to partially protect a soldier hugging the ground during an enemy bombardment. The grid points of every artillery unit, their respective motor pools and ammunition dumps, along with armor, infantry, and air defense elements and each major command headquarters at Camp Casey and nearby Camp Hovey were suspected to be well known by North Korean artillery spotters, so it was best to keep a safe distance, if and when.

(The 2nd Division has since been pulled from the line, deployed further south from the DMZ, but the ROK Army has taken over many of the U.S. compounds.)

The Division rarely practiced air raids . . . there was no need to. At the first shout of "Incoming!" by instinct everyone would "hit the dirt" then scramble for the ditches. The newbies would catch on quick or never know what hit them.

A nearby rock quarry (between Casey and Hovey) was used for demolitions practice and excavations by army combat engineers. The frequent blasting day and night echoed off the surrounding hills and throughout the Division headquarters area, and the emotional effect of each initial blast was heart-stopping.

Conversations paused mid-sentence, a noisy office suddenly fell silent as everyone wondered where the explosion came from. Infantrymen patrolling the surrounding mountains would halt in their tracks to feel the ground tremble and rumble. They'd wait. Was it just another excavation project, or was it the real thing, the opening salvo to a North Korean attack?

They anticipated the scream of an incoming artillery round, and quickly looked for a hole to dive into or dirt mound to hide behind, yet no one made a hasty move, not wishing to look foolish if it was just those damned engineers blowing things up again.

The wait lasted a few more seconds until everyone was assured the alert siren wasn't going off, but during that time everyone's mind was racing . . . some said a quick prayer, others remembered that it had been a while since they called home to talk to loved ones, a few relished the idea of possibly going to war, to flex their muscles and "show Joe Chink that he's picked the wrong Army to mess with."

At night just one dynamite charge from the rock quarry could postpone an eight-hour sleep as a GI realized enemy guns were locked on target for Division headquarters, and every other compound in the 2nd Division area.

A child's bedtime nursery rhyme took on a different perspective when intertwined with our own thoughts (after being jarred awake by one of those explosions, and kept awake the rest of the night by rattling windows). I couldn't help but think about the potential of another war during my 15-month tour in Korea:

JOURNAL: 359 DAYS LEFT

"Now I lay me down to sleep."
I hope all hell doesn't break loose tonight.
"I pray the Lord my soul to keep."
Damn, the DMZ's only a few miles away
*   and we're easily within range.*
"If I die before I wake, I pray the Lord my soul to take."
And I hope my family knows I love them.

JOURNAL: PHOTO OPS DURING OFF-DUTY TIME

When I was stationed at Yongsan in downtown Seoul, I could come and go every night and on weekends, so I spent every opportunity getting to know the beautiful people of Korea, the Land of the Morning Calm. Drugs and drinking and sneaking local girls into the barracks was quite rampant, and so to get away from all that, I spent most of my time at the Tender Apples Children's Home. But I also taught conversational English to KATUSA soldiers and college students, and led a summer course on newspaper design. With so many newfound friends, they often invited me to see the sites.

During my second tour in Korea, I was with the 2nd Infantry Division, up near the DMZ and getting a weekend pass was not always available. But when I did change into civilian clothes and left the compound, I always had my cameras with me, and ended up shooting more than 10,000 photos. I would often hop on a bus or a train and just ride until I spotted something interesting, then get off at the next stop and wander around for a few hours. I wasn't so much interested in the tourist stops, but in places the typical soldier wouldn't get to see.

None of these photos have anything to do with the DMZ or being a soldier stationed in Korea, but just maybe they do show why I love this country and its people, and why it's so important to do whatever I can to protect them from the ever-present threat from the north.

Sometimes at night, while the kids at the Tender Apples Children's Home did their homework, I would go to the roof and shoot photos of the surrounding neighborhood, including these two boys. Photo by Gary L. Bloomfield.

Thousands carrying paper lanterns converged on the local temples for Buddha's birthday. I started to take photos of this monk, but a young man rushed up and explained that the simple act of shooting a photo freezes his life for that split second, which I fully understood and put my camera down, but then he further explained that, for a small donation to the temple, I could shoot all the photos I wanted! Photo by Gary L. Bloomfield.

The Seoul marketplace is a bounty of fruits and vegetables, meat and fish . . . while North Koreans are starving, and scavenging for anything to eat. Photo by Gary L. Bloomfield.

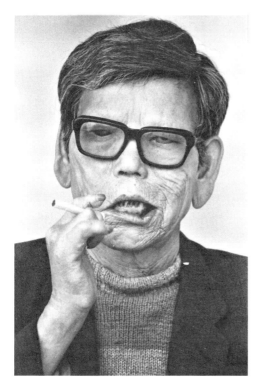

I had heard that there was a leper colony in central Korea, so I wanted to visit there and possibly write about it. Three days after the feature appeared in our post newspaper, the 121st Evacuation Hospital commander summoned me to his office and promptly informed me that every six months for the next ten years I would have to take a blood test. Photo by Gary L. Bloomfield.

She wore a deep purple sweater and was surrounded by light purple flowers. It was her husband's favorite color. Spent all day at the National Cemetery in Seoul, mourning him, who died in Vietnam, a year earlier.

I entered this photo in a contest when the movie Under Fire came out, and it won first place and an Olympus camera and lenses. Photo by Gary L. Bloomfield.

WHY ARE WE IN KOREA?

Tear the limbs off the U.S. beast. Behead it all over the world.
—Former North Korean leader Kim Il Sung

South Korea today is a vibrant, robust economy, a leader in not just Asia but the world, a majestic phoenix rising from the ashes of the Korean War. America has maintained a vital presence on the peninsula since the Armistice Agreement was signed in 1953. Every now and then there are serious discussions about the role American troops play in the region, and whether or not they are really necessary to maintain the shaky "peace" that exists between the north and the south.

When candidate for President Jimmy Carter announced his plans to withdraw troops in the mid-1970s, many soldiers already in country felt the effects of the "Vietnam syndrome"—the belief that the pullout of U.S. ground troops would be an open invitation for North Korea to invade the south. So why then, if South Korea will eventually fall under Communist rule, do American combat units bother to remain in Korea? Should they ever consider leaving if their presence is a key factor in deterring an invasion by the Communist north?

ASSESSING THE SITUATION

One senior military commander stationed in South Korea, after sensing skepticism among his troops, wrote the following letter to his subordinate unit commanders so they would understand the rationale of administration decisions affecting the U.S. military forces in Korea.

"In my brief period of command duty here I have heard from several sources, chiefly from the members of combat units, the questions, 'Why are we here?' and 'What are we fighting for?' What follows represents my answers to these questions.

"This command intends to maintain a military position in Korea just as long as the statesmen of the United Nations decide we should do so.

"The second question is of much greater significance. The real issues are whether the power of Western civilization, as God has permitted it to flower in our own beloved lands, shall defy and defeat Communism; whether the rule of men who shoot their prisoners, enslave their citizens, and deride the dignity of man, shall displace the rule of those to whom the individual and his individual rights are sacred; whether we are to survive with God's hand to guide and lead us, or to perish in the dead existence of a Godless world."

Those comments were excerpts from a letter by Army Lieutenant General M. B. Ridgway in 1951, and he was in the midst of rallying his troops to a mission, a war, many questioned at the time. Even for years after, the U.S. commitment is to ensure that South Korea does not "perish in the dead existence of a Godless world." The validity of America's "big brother" status is still as strong today as it was more than half century ago.

JOURNAL: 107 DAYS LEFT

Visited Inchon seawall today with Galen Geer. Tried to take photos of the anti-invasion devices during low tide, but a Korean Army soldier quickly approached and aimed his rifle in our direction. Told him we were sightseeing. We quickly got the hint but tried to find another location to get the photos.

Had Galen distract him by pulling out a tattered *Playboy* magazine. The guard quickly forgot about me and my camera. Ten minutes later I approached them, having shot two rolls of color film. The guard glared at me, knowing he'd been conned. I just smiled and gave him a pack of Winstons for his "cooperation." He also asked for the *Playboy*.

Desolate looking place, similar to DMZ. Nice place to visit, but . . .

Lieutenant General Matthew Ridgway in Korea, in April 1951. More than sixty years ago, he explained the importance of America's presence in South Korea. That stance is just as important today. Army photo.

JOURNAL: THANKSGIVING DAY

At a time of year when guns of battle echo loudly in other corners of the world, let us give thanks that ours, though poised and ever-ready, remain silent. Though we are far away from those we love we need not worry for they are safe and secure, away from this uncertainty we feel every day.

At times like this, when loneliness finds a soft spot, we may wonder why we're here? To the south, the people of the Land of the Morning Calm look to us as guardians of freedom. Sometimes publicly, often silently, they give thanks that we stand ready. Rock solid.

And even though our mission here is to fight, and keep on fighting, let us give thanks that for now our guns are silent.

JOURNAL: 103 DAYS LEFT

Everyone's noticed some odd occurrences throughout the Division during the past week. When put together these mean nothing less than an anticipated but dreaded North Korean attack on the south.

All liberty passes for all soldiers in the combat units were pulled, meaning everyone is restricted to the compound. In some units they can't even leave the company area. We've had three alerts in eight days, usually it's just one a month. For two of these alerts we drew weapons and ammunition, and moved out in the middle of the night.

Everyone is hush-hush in the headquarters area, which always means something big, that no one is allowed to talk about, is going to happen. But those of us who aren't privy to the upper echelons of secrecy and planning can only speculate, and eavesdrop whenever possible to gather morsels of information.

Normally all vehicles, tanks, artillery pieces, etc., are kept on line in motor pools that would be highly visible to enemy aircraft and copters. But now infantry, armor and artillery units have left the area, deploying to more strategic locations. They've nestled into the surrounding foothills all along the invasion corridors.

The command group has been concerned that the gas shortage is affecting our combat readiness. Quite possibly the North Koreans know about our limited gas supply, and plan to attack, thinking the Division is stalled. Do they know about our underground fuel reservoirs? Have they planned on sabotaging them?

The constant flow of news media visitors has been stopped indefinitely. Usually we escort them to prearranged training sites in the Division and often up to the DMZ, but now they can't even get inside the main gate, huddling there like a pack of hungry dogs waiting to be fed, stopping everyone in uniform who passes, desperately trying to get a brief sound bite they can expand on for the evening news back home.

For the first time I've been hearing a lot of talk about evacuation plans for women soldiers and dependent wives and children. Before, it had always been dictated that they would have to remain here (unless they could get to Seoul on their own), but now the command group is afraid that too many soldiers would ensure that their family was safe and out of the line of fire, instead of deploying with their unit to ward off the invasion. And under no circumstances does anyone want to chance having an American female soldier fall into enemy hands.

Something's up, and it ain't good.

A LITTLE BLACK HUMOR

> Don't be scared. Every bullet has a name on it. If your name is not on, then you're safe. I'm worried about the bullet which has on it, "To whom it may concern."—Louis Nizer

"If the worst happens here [along the DMZ], if the North Koreans invade again, there'll be a lot of Americans killed. We'll lose an infantry battalion right off. I want my men to remember that."

At the time, the specific unit Major General Morris J. Brady, former 2nd Infantry Division commander in the mid-1970s, was referring to is the Z Battalion, the 2/9th Infantry "Manchus" (which have since withdrawn from South Korea and returned home). But as long as the Indianhead Division remained deployed between Seoul and the DMZ, there would always be one unit designated as the Z Battalion.

Their mission was to hold Freedom Bridge in event of an enemy attack, that all-too-vital focal point, a crossroads between freedom and "life-sucking" Communism, that if destroyed would seal the fate of hundreds of American soldiers trapped on the northern bank of the Imjin River.

"We're here to protect and evacuate the Americans and United Nations Command personnel inside the Joint Security Area at PanMunJom," stated one Manchu private, a border guard, when asked about his twelve-month mission on the DMZ. It would take approximately ten to fifteen minutes to drive as quickly as possible from the Joint Security Area to the southern side of Freedom Bridge in the event of a North Korean attack. The same young private noted a little black humor in that seemingly not-so-important and easy to accomplish fact.

"Officials figure we've got less than eleven minutes to get across the bridge before North Korean artillery can get an accurate fix and blow it. That's not counting however long it takes to evacuate everyone from PanMunJom. That's no sweat to get across if you've got wheels, or maybe a head start, but

Two soldiers on patrol along the Southern Barrier Fence in the mid-1970s, as the sun sets. As members of the Z Battalion, they knew that if the North Koreans invaded the south, they would never make it to safety before being overrun. Photo by Gary L. Bloomfield.

JOURNAL: 39 DAYS LEFT

Stopped at the southern shore of the Imjin River to take pictures of Freedom Bridge. Military Police immediately blocked our path and refused to allow any pix. Drove slowly across single-lane, wooden planks and shot through the windshield instead. Noticed explosive charges and detonation wires along the full length of the bridge.

Drove to Camp Greaves (headquarters for the 2/9th Infantry Battalion). Took seven minutes from the bridge. It would be impossible for foot soldiers to run to the bridge in time. They all seem to understand and accept their fate.

the Z Battalion, we're all ground-pounders. We walk, everywhere, and that bridge is about three miles away. No way we could get there in eleven minutes, even in a flat-out sprint for our lives. You want to know the real reason we're here?

"We serve as sitting ducks so they can wipe us out, an entire U.S. Army battalion, several hundred men, which would automatically commit the United States to war. Funny . . . isn't it?"

GOOD LUCK CHARMS AND SUPERSTITIONS

Most service members who deploy to a war zone or even a hostile fire zone like the Korean DMZ realize that any day could be their last. For some, those combatants who venture forth and face the fiery dragon on a daily basis, the odds of surviving unscathed is stacked even higher against them. Some are willing to tempt fate and thumb their nose at the widow maker, (or defiantly flip him off!), believing they're invincible, but many more look for any edge to tilt the scales back in their favor.

Maybe it's visiting the unit chaplain for a special prayer of safe passage, a prayer they've said a hundred times before, and will keep saying it for another two hundred. It might be a quiet conversation with a loved one who's thousands of miles away, or eating a bowl of cereal with sliced fruit before heading out beyond the perimeter walls, wearing a dirty smelly T-shirt for every foot patrol because no one's been injured whenever it's been worn, maybe tapping their weapon five times and clicking their heals another five. Maybe it's eating one red licorice stick every day before heading out, or . . . actually it really doesn't matter what it is. If they believe it'll keep them out of danger, then to hell with what anyone else thinks.

They may not openly admit it, but many warriors also carry good luck charms of some sort—inspirational quotes, lucky tokens, religious medallions, family photos, Bible verses, talismans of questionable origins—to keep them safe from harm and ward off the dragon. Many also believe if they don't have their good luck charms with them, or they forget to do that insignificant ritual, their day is going to turn ugly, absolutely, no doubt about it.

Whatever it is—some small trinket or medallion, some simple ritual which means nothing to anyone else—it helps these combatants to survive in a combat zone, for just one more day, in a string of days of danger and uncertainty. And most of the time, they get to the end of their day, they come back from another patrol or another sleepless night in the observation tower inside the DMZ, just happy they had their good luck charm with them.

Some days, they're not so lucky, and no amount of praying, no misplaced good luck charm left behind somewhere, would change the outcome of a really bad day. Sadly, too often those bad days are their last days among the living.

> Professional soldiers are sentimental men, for all the harsh realities of their calling. In their wallets and in their memories they carry bits of philosophy, fragments of poetry, quotations from the Scriptures, which, in times of stress and danger speak to them with great meaning. —General Matthew B. Ridgway in *My Battles in War and Peace*, 1956

COMBATANTS SHARE THEIR TALISMANS

"I carried a brass medallion with the Lord's Prayer engraved on it. Never needed to look at it because I knew the Prayer by heart, but every time I went out on patrol, I would pull it out and rub it for good luck, convincing myself that no harm would come to me or my guys as long as I had that with me."

"The common joke is that it's not the stray bullet that's going to kill you. It's the one with your name on it. Knowing that, I carried a bullet with my name engraved on it, figuring that if I had it buttoned in my pocket, it couldn't kill me."

"I'm a medic. Didn't carry good luck charms, but I made sure to pack safety pins, Super Glue and tampons . . . the latter to plug bullet holes until we could get the guy back to the aid station."

"My mom was the worry wart in our family. She wasn't happy unless she was worrying about someone. Gave me the Lord's Prayer at the airport, which I kept in my wallet, and wanted me to say it every day, even if we didn't go out on patrol, but I usually stopped before the end of it and changed it just a little—

'Our Father who art in heaven, hallowed be thy name. Thy kingdom come. Thy will be done, on Earth as it is in Heaven. Give us this day, our daily bread. And forgive us our debts, as we forgive our debtors. And lead us not into temptation, but deliver us from evil . . . for I am the meanest SOB in the Kingdom.' Yeah, but my mom probably wouldn't appreciate my version of it, so . . ."

"Spent Thanksgiving at home for the first time in five years. Got the wishbone and brought it with me. I figure if we get into a hairy situation, I'll pull that thing out, make a wish and hope things turn out okay. Of course in the meantime I'll put my weapon on full auto and empty the clip."

"I'm an Army brat of an Army brat. Been in for ten years and carry the dog tags my grandfather carried in the Korean War and which he gave to my dad before he shipped out to 'Nam, and now they're mine, to keep me safe."

"As I was packing to ship out, my son kept asking all sorts of questions, and couldn't understand why I had to go, and couldn't grasp how long a year was. I explained that I had to go, to protect the world from bad people. When I got to my unit and unpacked my duffel bag, there inside was my son's plastic Texas Rangers badge . . . so I could arrest the bad guys."

"I went straight from Iraq to Korea, which was a piece of cake compared to. . . . So anyway I get home and dump my duffel bag in the corner of the living room and sleep all weekend. I wake up Monday midday and my wife is pissed, though I'm not sure why. I'm thinking it's because I've been gone so long, but I go out to the kitchen and there on the table are three condoms I'd left in my BDU pants pocket. I tried explaining that in Iraq we had sand storms all the time so we'd put a condom on the end of our muzzle—the muzzle of our weapon—to keep the sand out. In Korea, I still did it when we went out on patrols, especially during the rainy season. She didn't believe me, so she calls one of the other wives, who asks her husband about the condoms. He confirms my story, but she doesn't believe him either, so now we're both in the doghouse."

"I didn't have a good luck charm, but I knew this second lieutenant who fer sure was OCD. Every time we went out on patrol, he'd give us a briefing—about suspected enemy activity, any changes to the rules of engagement, etc.—then he'd end it with 'Hoo-Ah,' expecting us to say it back. Usually we weren't paying any attention, but then he'd pretend like there was something else he forgot to tell us, then do the 'Hoo-Ah' thing again, so then we'd intentionally not answer back. A more senior officer might order us to say it, but he was such a baby-face wuss, he'd just keep blabbering on with more nonsense, until finally the first sergeant would step in and dismiss us, leaving the looney lieutenant flustered the rest of the day."

"I had a corded bright blue bracelet. No one knew but my wife had taken one of her thongs, and braided the cords into a bracelet and tied it to my wrist, as a constant reminder of what was waiting for me when I got home."

JOURNAL

The first time I was deployed to Korea was just two weeks after I'd gotten married. My good luck charm was my wife's garter belt from the wedding.

The second time I got sent to Korea, my daughter was just a year and a half old. I was really afraid she wouldn't remember me when I got back a year later. I kept a photo of the three of us together and wondered how much she would change the next time I saw her.

PRAY FOR HIM

You want to be brave. You also want to be. —Peter Bowman

Despite the falsehood of peace guaranteed by the Armistice Agreement, U.S. forces in South Korea are prepared to go to war at a moment's notice. And frequent border clashes along the DMZ with North Korean infiltrators support the basis for keeping the "combat" designation, despite the common belief among Americans back home that the peninsula has had decades of peace, with minor hiccups every now and then, but nothing approaching the brink of war, or so they want to believe.

Even after U.S. troops were pulled off the DMZ and stationed further south, the border incidents have continued, between ROK and DPRK guards.

More than six decades have passed since the signing of the "truce" agreement, calling an end to the Korean War, but the United States has had to pay heavily since then to maintain an uneasy peace in South Korea. More than forty thousand truce violations have been documented at the continuing "peace" talks. And more than 1,200 American, South Korean and North Korean soldiers have been killed in and along the "cease-fire" zone.

Those statistics are hard to ignore, yet somehow they've been kept from the American public. As a result, when a family is notified that their boy is killed in Korea, it's hard to understand the sense of it all, especially since they erroneously thought "there's no war going on there, right?"

In 1950, the popular commentator Walter Winchell made a statement about American soldiers that's been appropriate all these many years. Unfortunately many people don't realize how true his statement is, until they're weeping silently at a military funeral for their son, or their husband, or their father . . . a fallen soldier killed along Korea's Demilitarized Zone.

Winchell's comment was chilling for more than five decades:

> If you have a son overseas, write to him.
> If you have a son in the 2nd Division . . . pray for him.
> If you have a son in the 2nd Division . . . pray for him.

Fool me once, shame on you; fool me twice, shame on me.
—Chinese proverb

They often look crazy to us because they use what has been called "karate diplomacy." They try to catch opponents off guard with sudden moves. —Selig Harrison, author of *Korean Endgame*

I like old Marx Brothers movies and I think it was "Duck Soup" in which Groucho points a gun at his head and says "Stop, Stop or I'll shoot!" which is pretty much the foreign policy of North Korea. —Retired Colonel Ken Allard, military analyst

JOURNAL: 17 DAYS LEFT

Tomorrow I will journey into the DMZ for a final time before I return home. I've lost track of how many trips I've made there. One more shouldn't really matter that much. But every time, as we approach the Southern Barrier Fence, I say a little prayer to myself—"Lord watch over me" and hope he's not sleeping on the job.

Have to write another letter home. Just in case.

• 22 •

Deciphering the Myths
of the Kim Dynasty

$\mathcal{O}$ften the so-called news reports coming out of Pyongyang are little more than puff pieces, intent on glorifying the unbelievable accomplishments and back story of the triumvirate of the Kim dynasty—founder Kim Il Sung, his son Kim Jong Il and the latest Kim, grandson Jong Un. Separating fact from fantasy may be easier to do from a distance, but for the North Korean masses—who are not privy to the Internet or broadcasts outside of state-run TV (and smuggled in videos of South Korean soap operas)—it would be easy to assume the Kims are mythical gods personified . . . a holy trinity of amazing feats. Certainly no mortal man could accomplish what they have done—

- Kim Il Sung single-handedly defeated the Japanese during World War II, and vanquished the American, South Korean, and United Nations forces during the Korean War, according to the well-known history of North Korea. In a speech on April 15, 2012, Kim Jong Un admitted that his grandfather "performed the military miracle of the 20th Century of defeating the two most outrageous imperialisms in one generation." Simply having the largest statues in the world qualifies Kim Il Sung for sainthood. (Okay so maybe the busts on Mount Rushmore might be bigger, but there's only one Mount Rushmore. There are countless statues of the mighty Kim throughout the country.) Not just satisfied with a few hundred statues of himself, Kim and his son ordered the construction of more than thirty-five thousand, mostly funded with misappropriated aid money intended to ease the suffering of the North Korean people. It has even been claimed that he never used the bathroom, because he was a perfect God and had no need for basic human functions.

Despite being one of the most impoverished countries in the world, North Korea spends millions to glorify the Kim dynasty and their supposed unbelievable accomplishments. DPRK News Service.

- Kim Jong Il was born in February 1942, on Mount Paedku, Korea's highest peak, or so his fictitious bio states. A star streaked across the sky, a glacier split, followed by a double rainbow, a new star suddenly appeared in the heavens, the seasons immediately changed from harsh Winter to glorious life-affirming Spring and cranes flew across the land, heralding the arrival of this fortunate son. Every school child in North Korea knows his story and bows to the images of the Kims, displayed in every room. In reality he was born in 1941, at an army base near Khabarovsk, in the Russian territories, when his father led Korean soldiers against the Japanese. Even though the war ended when he was four, North Korean propaganda claims the younger Kim was a brave fighter, serving alongside his father in vanquishing the Japanese.

"I should explain that the name Kim Jong Il is written with three characters that mean 'a Truly Golden Sun,'" wrote Christopher Buckley in the article "Field of Screams," for *Forbes*, Winter 2002. An avid fan of western flicks—most notably James Bond and Rambo films and Daffy Duck cartoons (that alone says a lot—qualified Kim Jong Il as an expert at film making, which he parlayed into overseeing North Korea's propaganda machine, resulting in thousands of movies, plays, operas, and songs glorifying his father). In the "believe it or not" category, he played a round of golf exactly one time in his life, and yet he pulled off the impossible feat of sinking five holes-in-one.

There is no world-ranked golfer, past or present, who has managed that little rarity, except for maybe playing miniature golf. Kim Jong Il was such an avid sportsman and knowledgeable expert on basketball that he decreed everyone should play basketball, in order to grow taller.

(Hate to break the news, but due to wide-spread famine and years of malnutrition, the average North Korean child is inches shorter and many pounds lighter than their South Korean counterpart, who is more inclined to play video games than basketball.) While millions of his countrymen were starving, Kim Jong Il diverted aid money and the profits from various counterfeiting activities to guzzle Hennessey Cognac. (Might as well pickle the liver with the best!) "He was Hennessey's largest single paying customer. This man liked his good food," stated author Michael Breen. "It's the kind of evil where there's no feeling. There's just emptiness. Those starving people howling out there mean nothing."

Kim Jong Il was such a connoisseur of elegant dining, it was claimed he even invented the hamburger (not that any of his countrymen outside of Pyongyang would ever taste such a delicacy. They're just lucky if they get to have a small portion of meat once a year.)

- Kim Jong Un was driving at the tender age of three, and at nine, navigated a yacht to victory against an accomplished yacht builder. Little else is known about his childhood, other than he went to school in Switzerland, and only returned to Pyongyang when he was being groomed to take over when his father died. Past accomplishments are still being conjured up by the North Korean propaganda mill. Almost as soon as he ascended to the throne, he was labeled a brilliant military tactician, without any military training or experience. On his birthday in 2012, a documentary labeled him as "the genius among the geniuses" for his "excellent military leadership," claiming that even at the tender age of sixteen, he wrote his first thesis on military strategy. While sleeping less than four hours a night and skipping meals to crack the books, he feverishly wrote his thesis, knowing someday he would share his brilliance with the military commanders he would soon lead to the brink of the abyss. (And anyone who opposes him is imprisoned or used for target practice.) The documentary proclaimed him the "spitting image" of his grandfather, the revered Kim Il Sung, worthy to stand by him in both personality and leadership.

While not considered one of Kim Jong Un's own personal accomplishments, it has been told that his guidance of North Korea's long-range missile development has led to one of the most outlandish claims. The Korea Central

JOURNAL

I've written two books on General George Patton, who believed in reincarnation, and in previous lives, had served alongside many of the great commanders, such as Alexander and Hannibal, Peter and Napoleon, Caesar and Sherman. It might be far-fetched but I guess little Kim could have studied his grandfather's military "successes" and strategies via osmosis or even standing at his side, in a past life. How else could he qualify as a military genius?

News Agency proclaimed: "We are very delighted to announce a successful mission to put a man on the sun. North Korea has beaten every other country in the world to the sun. Hung Il Gong is a hero and deserves a hero's welcome when he returns home later this evening."

Supposedly Hung, Il Gong, at just seventeen and a nephew of Kim Jong Un, made the journey in just four hours, though it took another eighteen to return. (Some say this story is a hoax intended to embarrass North Korea, but what is known is that, without access to the Internet or outside news sources, many North Koreans do believe everything they hear and that it is possible to land a man on the sun.)

What is totally baffling to most outsiders pulling back the curtains and trying to get a peek inside the craziness and zaniness of the Kim regime is the outpouring of loyalty and devotion from all North Koreans, despite the imprisonment of thousands for bogus charges, and the starvation of millions.

When Kim Il Sung died in 1994, the mass hysteria of grief overwhelmed the entire country, though skeptics wondered if the overblown theatrics were genuine. "There is no doubt that for the majority of North Koreans, his death came as a very unpleasant shock. The initial outpouring of grief from large urban centers to the smallest villages was very real indeed, even though the prolongation of the grieving period gave way to more contrived, theatrical expressions," wrote Erich Weingartner, on January 5, 2012, for 38North, a project of the U.S.-Korea Institute. "By the time of the funeral, ten days later, much of the weeping would have become standard issue conformity. It would look bad not to show one's grief on a national day of mourning. It would not be a good example for one's children if the parents do not show proper respect for their ancestors or the country's leaders. And beyond that, during a period of uncertainty, it would not be wise to stick out like a sore thumb."

Whether or not the outpouring of grief is truly genuine is debatable. In a recent documentary, the narrator noticed that during the funeral for Kim Jong Il, solemn mourners watched passively as the funeral procession passed by, but as soon as they spotted the TV camera approaching they started wailing hysterically. Then once the camera had moved on, the theatrics stopped.

In a country where everyone watches everyone else for any little misstep, anyone who doesn't show the appropriate amount of respect for the Great Leader, or the Dear Leader or the Supreme Leader, is reported and promptly hauled off to a prison camp for "re-education."

In *Foreign Policy* magazine, Thomas Ricks and Lieutenant General Daniel P. Bolger cautioned, in the May 2, 2017, issue: "North Korea is all about the Kims. Everything north of the DMZ trace is designed to keep this strange family in power. Joseph Stalin is the model for these guys, and in their endless devotion to propaganda, purges, and prison camps, the Kims have proven at least as paranoid and vicious as evil old Uncle Joe. Kim Jong Un will do whatever it takes to keep his regime. He saw what became of Manuel Noriega, Saddam Hussein, and Moammar Qaddafi. That's not where Kim Jong Un intends to end up."

"If you study relations between North Korea and the United States, you'll spend a lot of time reading propaganda, trying to parse phrases for evidence of internal political disputes or perhaps to discern a subtle shift in policy. It can be a chore to sort through the immense amount of tendentious nonsense coming from one of the world's least transparent governments, trying to figure out exactly what the heck they are thinking," wrote Jeffrey Lewis in the article "Inside the Dread Box: Seeking Policy in Propaganda," on May 21, 2014, for 38North, a project of the U.S.-Korea Institute at Johns Hopkins School of Advanced International Studies based in Washington, D.C.

Neither Kim Il Sung before, his son or grandson have ever shown much concern for outside opinion, except maybe from Beijing and Moscow, and, as such, make their own rules of international "diplomacy" as they go bumbling along. "If you look at their track record of fifty years, they are lunatics . . . cunning and calculating," cautioned James Lilley, former U.S. ambassador to South Korea.

"They have to go around the world with a begging bowl, showing pictures of starving children," explained Ambassador Lilley. "The trouble is, we know perfectly well that probably the top 50 percent of their food supplies goes right to their Army" and not to the elderly, the women and those children who are starving to death. Plus, with the dismantling of the Soviet sphere into numerous satellites, each struggling to make it on their own, the dwindling handouts cannot meet the demands of the desperate North Korean military, let alone its civilian populace.

Whether he continues to threaten a nuclear "firestorm" or wises up and realizes his only option for regime survival is to negotiate in good faith with the United States, South Korea and his other neighbors, Kim Jong Un is getting boxed into a corner, in an impossible position.

Final Thoughts

If a man says he intends to attack you, fully prepares to do so and has done so in the past, then presumably you act on the assumption that he means it. —Ivan Barnes, foreign news editor, *The Times of London*, 1976

This might lose a little in the translation but Nathan Bedford Forrest had a message that still rings true: *Get 'em skeered and keep the skeer on 'em.*

*W*hile stationed with the 2nd Infantry Division, I had been a part of the military press corps in South Korea that downplayed the incidents taking place along the Demilitarized Zone. I had escorted media representatives to the front, stood close and listened to their probing questions and sometimes incessant badgering put to 2nd Division soldiers. Then I later read the stories that were filed by these unsuspecting reporters or saw their broadcasts, and they all had thought they had gotten a true picture of the goings-on at the front. Did they ever realize that we had briefed each of these soldiers on what to say? More importantly, even without our prompting, these Indianhead warriors knew what not to say, what not to let anyone know about.

On other occasions Galen Geer and I had visited the truce zone for features we wanted to do—such as spending Christmas at Guard Post Ouellette, or checking out the mystery of Lookout Post #5—and we talked with other soldiers and officers stationed there. Unlike the civilian press though, we were free to roam the southern sector of the DMZ at will, so if at any time a commander had pointed us toward a specific group of soldiers, we'd turn the opposite way and seek out others who maybe weren't as articulate, but they sure had plenty to say.

Their stories were eye-opening, often hard to imagine, quite possibly passed down and elaborated on over the years (and in some of the more ridiculous cases, impossible for Galen or me to verify and so I discarded them for this book), but the factuality of their comments were not of utmost importance to us. What did concern us was their perceptions of the incidents they told us about, and what we were reading in the daily situation reports at 2nd Division headquarters and in the local Korean newspapers. Right or wrong, exaggerated or not, what they believed to be true and how they dealt with that information was what we were seeking. Some admitted they prayed to God they wouldn't become a statistic, one of the thousands of "truce violations."

One soldier at a remote guard post always wore a thick metal band around his neck (and kept it hidden under a camouflaged scarf) whenever it was his turn for sentry duty at night, because he'd heard that several American soldiers had been found with their throat slit in that same post he was manning at the time (Post #5 at Ouellette).

Another GI always insisted on sleeping in the top rack of a bunk bed. His reasoning? Several years prior, North Korean infiltrators had planted explo-

Part of our public affairs duties was documenting visiting dignitaries when they toured the DMZ. 2nd Division commander, Major General David Grange, squatting, briefs Army Chief of Staff, General Bernard Rogers, while at Guard Post Ouellette. Both seemed indifferent to their proximity to North Korea, just yards from the perimeter fence, beyond which snipers could be lurking. Photo by Gary L. Bloomfield.

sive charges under an American troop billets near the DMZ. When the blasts occurred, two GIs were killed and several others injured. If the stunt was to ever be repeated, this particular soldier wanted at least the floor, the bottom mattress, another guy sleeping on it, and his own mattress between him and the explosion.

Still another soldier always carried a cigarette pack filled with plastic explosives and a trip switch in his pocket whenever he went on a patrol inside the DMZ. He had been told that whenever North Korean infiltrators ambush an American patrol, they always check the bodies for jewelry, money, and cigarettes. If he was to die, at least knowing the cigarette pack would blow up in some North Korean's face would be sweet revenge.

Three GIs that Galen and I had met at the Z. They each had their own quirks, they each found their own way to cope with living in the Devil's Playground. They each believed the stories they'd heard that impacted on their own little corner of the edge of the world. Whether or not these stories had any validity didn't matter to the soldiers who stayed awake at night wondering if their tour in Korea, twelve months of uncertainty, would pass without incident . . . if they would ever see loved ones again. The vast majority put in their time and returned home safely. But there were the few . . .

I recall a handful of sleepless nights while serving with the Indianhead Division. Certainly being back at Division headquarters wasn't as perilous as spending day and night on the DMZ but, like the soldiers I'd interviewed, I couldn't merely brush aside the stories they'd told me without feeling some shred of truth there. Later, during years of research, I've found additional documented incidents even worse than the gossip that filtered along the DMZ, the stories we'd heard.

For many of the soldiers stationed there on the Korean DMZ, whether pulling a one-month rotation, or a twelve-month stint, it's a time they never forget. Geoffrey Porter was with the 2nd of the 38th Infantry. Even forty years later he remembers: "The life of a soldier has always been different in fundamental ways from that of a civilian and always will be, and can only be understood by living it. The best memories I have are of the wonderful friends I made living in some very primitive conditions. We were young and tough because we had to be. Almost a year later when I rotated back to the States it took some adjustment for me as I was so accustomed to a very different world.

"I was half way around the world living a very different life, learning a very different culture. Most of us had a fairly good time despite some of the conditions. Deep down inside, I think we all knew that we were living an adventure. As young troops we lived together, worked together, ate together and relaxed together. We shared our troubles, our fears, our jokes, and teased each other. We all looked out for each other. Later, when we were back out of the field and in garrison, life resumed a more familiar pattern. Then, one morning just after the morning PT run, I saw a close buddy in his dress greens outside the orderly room with his duffel bag. He was on his way to the Turtle Farm (Transfer Point) for rotation back home to another assignment. You shake hands, slap backs, and laugh, promising to keep in touch, then he's gone.

"Looking through some mementoes not too long ago, I found an old shoulder patch from an old uniform, the 2nd Division Indianhead patch. How fortunate I was to have served with such fine Americans. You know, I haven't seen the guys I knew back then for over forty years, but I will always miss them."

This book, originally written between 1977 and 1980 while I was still in the Army as a photojournalist, had to be cleared by a variety of agencies in Washington, D.C., including the Pentagon, the National Security Agency, and the State Department, with much of it stamped "classified" and so it could not be used in this updated version.

Field training exercises, such as Team Spirit, and live fire exercises were great opportunities for photos, and to talk with combat soldiers.
The commander for this M60 mentioned that he had seen a photo of the muzzle flash and suggested I try it. I initially thought if I stood near the rear treads I could get the muzzle flash and the shell leaving the barrel. Instead, I got knocked on my ass . . . several times before I moved away a few yards, then a few yards more, until finally, I got the shot.
Photo by Gary L. Bloomfield.

Because of that, it may not have been in the best interests of foreign policy at that time (when that whole issue of troop withdrawal was being considered) to have it published.

And by the way, it was because of President Carter's campaign pledge to withdraw troops from the region that I felt the need to write this book, to explain to the American public just how vital and vulnerable South Korea was at that time.

Now it is forty years later and once again, that cauldron known as North Korea is threatening to boil over, and many are surprised. I'm not sure why though. It has always been a powder keg and North Korea's leadership—whether it's Kim Il Sung the former or his son, Kim Jong Il, or now the grandson—Kim Jong Un—seems to always be holding a lit match and waving it perilously close to the fuse, threatening to stand back and watch the fireworks . . . only now he's got nukes in his arsenal of play toys.

U.S. forces have had nukes in country for decades. In fact, while flipping through my journal notes for this update of *Devil's Playground*, I came across the following entries:

JOURNAL

As editor for the *Indianhead* newspaper, I had the task of showing the layout pages to the division CG before we went to press. I often wrote the front-page feature, and certainly edited everything and did all of the layouts. Occasionally Major General Brady wanted me to write specific stories and I was always amazed that these were about controversial issues, such as black market activity in the division area, and the local hospital which was doctoring the shot records of the "working girls" who were required to do VD checks every month, to name just two of the stories.

Most commanders want their newspaper to shy away from any hot topics, but General Brady wanted them addressed and for everyone in the command to know it. He read each page thoroughly and often suggested changes. The first few times, I would have to hustle back to my office, make the changes, then take them back, for him to approve, before taking the pages to the print plant. Eventually, he trusted me to make the changes without a re-look.

One time I was walking back from his office around mid-morning, when I saw our four KATUSAs standing outside our Quonset hut. From a distance I figured they were just smoking but as I got closer, I noticed they all had their boots and socks off and took turns doing the hokey-pokey, or some sort of little jig. They were standing in a square, and were taunting each other and tormenting something on the asphalt in the middle of them. From a few feet away, I noticed what looked like a six-inch snake. They asked if I wanted to join in, and said it was a "two-step snake."

I asked, "What's that?" They said if it bites, you'll take two steps and drop dead!

I politely declined, not really feeling the need to test my manhood just then. A few minutes later they all walked back inside, with their boots on. I didn't ask what they did with their pet.

On a larger scale, sometimes I wonder if North Korea likes taunting the more-powerful United States, seeing how much they can get away with, then backing off and waiting for our reaction.

The North Korean military and the civilian masses are brainwashed to believe they are just as powerful as the United States, and as such, continually underestimate what would happen if they push too far . . . if they play the hokey-pokey and the United States one day bites back. It would be a fatal mistake.

JOURNAL

Working late in the office. Everyone else left two hours ago. Probably at the clubs in TDC by now, getting snockered. Gotta get the layout pages done tonight since the CG wants to see them first thing in the morning. Hopefully he won't make too many changes, which would delay getting on the road to the print plant.

I heard the phone ring at the other end of the building, and I shoulda just ignored it, but whoever it was let it ring ten times then hung up, two minutes later it'd be ringing again, ten times. This went on for twenty minutes and I couldn't concentrate. I shoulda just taken the phone off the hook, but then foolishly I answered it.

"Hello, Matie. Hope I'm not bothering you?"

Immediately recognized the voice, but never knew his real name. We just called him Kangaroo Jack, foreign correspondent for one of the Aussie newspapers. Bothered us once a month for a DMZ story, then he'd go away for a few weeks.

Usually the PAO liked to deal with the reporters . . . no, that's not completely true. He didn't trust us to deal with the reporters . . . but I could at least find out what Jack wanted and give the boss a heads up in the morning.

"Me and the boys heard a rumor that you blokes in the 2nd Infantile gots nukes stashed away somewhere. Care to elaborate on that?"

Didn't even have to pause for a second to answer that one. "I can neither confirm nor deny that we have nuclear weapons in country."

"Geez Louise, Matie. They told me the exact same thing at Osan Air Base and Eighth Army HQ, word for word. Can't you do any better than that?"

"Sorry Jack. I can neither confirm nor deny that . . ."

"Yeah, yeah. I got it. One of my blokes in Melbourne heard that you guys have nuke land mines and hand grenades."

"I hadn't heard that one, Jack. What are they like, low yield, say maybe one mega-ton?" As soon as I said that I knew it would come back and bite me in the ass. We'd always been told never to say more than "I can neither confirm nor deny . . ." and that anything we did say was on the record, even if we were off duty.

"Yeah, one of them baby nukes. So, can I quote you on that?"

"Not in my lifetime."

"How 'bout if I just say a division spokesman?"

"How about if you just quote me as saying I can neither confirm nor deny that we have nuclear weapons in country? Better yet, why don't you call back in the morning and get an official statement from the PAO?"

"No need to, Matie. You just confirmed what I was wondering about."

I knew it wouldn't do any good to tap dance my way out of that. It would only make it worse. I just hoped the back blast wouldn't take too big a chunk outta my ass.

It did . . . two days later, when his story got disseminated in DOD's Early Bird, which is a compilation of newspaper and magazine clippings, speeches and transcripts from television reports, all pertaining to the military.

Twenty-five years earlier, General Douglas MacArthur wanted to unleash a nuke to put a quick end to the Korean War. The North Koreans, bolstered with thousands of ChiCom solders certainly knew it was a possibility. The wastelands of Hiroshima and Nagasaki were proof of that.

Though his country was destroyed by extensive carpet-bombing, Kim Il Sung never forgot the doomsday threat of a nuclear attack. And through the years, as other world powers joined the nuclear arms race, Kim sought to join the club, believing it would somehow give him some legitimacy on the world stage. It didn't, but he kept trying, as did his son and now his grandson.

In recent years I felt it was time to dig out the original *Devil's Playground* (curse a lot about all the excised pages, all the great stuff I couldn't use) and bring it all up to date. It ain't the finished piece I would like to have, but even without the censored deletions, I think the picture is still pretty damning.

Still, there are also many topics that are simply outside my lane, such as the famine that has devastated a vast majority of the population (those outside of Pyongyang); North Korea's numerous illegal enterprises to generate much-needed cash (such as producing counterfeit American money and counterfeit high-value drugs); providing weapons and munitions to rogue nations and terrorist groups; diverting the millions of dollars in aid to build up the military and cater to the privileged elites in Pyongyang; the thousands of defectors and the thousands more attempting to flee; the millions imprisoned for life and the countless more who have simply disappeared, many because they disrespected one of the Kims or because they were caught worshipping a Western religion.

Instead, my focus is the Demilitarized Zone over the past six-plus decades, and the men and women who have been stationed there.

"There's no war going on in Korea" many Americans believe. After leaving Vietnam, the battlegrounds sprang up in the Middle East, Kosovo, the Mog, Kuwait, Iraq, or Afghanistan. There was little room left on the front pages of the major newspapers for any mention of some trivial incident in Korea. But I had been there, and I knew there was more going on . . . even when there wasn't anything going on!

The American people remain in the dark regarding the Devil's Playground and the true intentions of North Korea to retake the south, by force if necessary. Despite any peace overtures coming out of Pyongyang, despite the sham of reconciliation and reunification, there is one crucial piece that no one must ever forget in dealing with North Korea: The vast majority of the population has been indoctrinated over many years to hate Americans and all we stand for.

The children of the fifties and sixties there are now stepping into leadership positions and they have not forgotten those lessons learned about so-called American brutality during the Korean War, they have not forgotten all the "heroes" of the cause who have killed Americans on the DMZ during these past sixty years, and they may still believe the greatest gift they could offer to their country's leadership is the killing of another American "imperialist."

That hatred, instilled over many, many years does not, has not dissipated.

It is now more than sixty years after the Armistice Agreement was signed. There's a new regime in Pyongyang and a no-nonsense American president with the backbone to finally negotiate a lasting peace which will benefit all of Northeast Asia, a region with three of the most vibrant and prosperous countries in the world, and one on life support. Much has been done in recent months to defuse the tensions, but it's too early to know if in fact, North Korea will join the world of civilized nations, or continue to edge closer to Armageddon, which is a certainty if they want to provoke a fight with the United States and South Korea.

Index

About the Author

Gary Bloomfield is an Army brat, and, like most military children, moved multiple times while growing up. He's lived in several states and overseas, including France and Germany, where he graduated from high school. Soon after returning to the states, he was drafted, and served for ten years in the Army, as a journalist, newspaper editor, photo-journalist, and video cameraman. He was also managing editor for *VFW* magazine and an Army public affairs supervisor in Kansas City, before retiring to write books full time.

Two weeks after marrying his high school sweetheart, he was sent to Korea for the first time, where he was editor for the *Profile* newspaper in Yongsan, in downtown Seoul. He spent most nights and weekends at the Tender Apples Childrens Home, rather than spend any time in the barracks. He also taught conversational English to ROK Army soldiers and local college students and taught newspaper layout and design to a college journalism class. He shot photos of Korean children for promotional materials for Foster Parents and Save the Children.

He returned to Korea in 1977 and served with the 2nd Infantry Division near the DMZ, as editor for the *Indianhead* newspaper. For his efforts during this tour, he was selected as the Army Journalist of the Year and U.S. Forces Korea Best Journalist. The *Indianhead* was also recognized as best newspaper in U.S. Forces Korea, and many of the articles were best in their categories. At the same time. He again taught conversational English to ROK Army soldiers and college students in Seoul.

At the same time, he started researching and writing *The Devil's Playground*. Because he was still in the military, he had to submit the manuscript to the Pentagon for clearance and approval. Six months later, the book was returned, with large sections redacted. If he wanted to make the necessary changes he would have to resubmit the book for clearance. By this time he was with the U.S. Army Europe News Team in Germany and left the book behind with his parents.

After ten years in the Army, he had to leave to take care of his parents. He got his bachelor's and master's degrees on the GI Bill, then worked as managing editor for *VFW* magazine in Kansas City. During the 50th anniversary of WWII, the magazine published recaps of the battles, then compiled these for two commemorative books: *Faces of Victory, Europe* and *Faces of Victory, Pacific*. Initially, he planned to write lengthy chapters on WWII entertainers and WWII athletes for these books, but space was limited so these chapters were excluded, but he kept doing research and in 2002 published *Duty, Honor, Victory: America's Athletes in WWII*, followed by *Duty, Honor, Applause. America's Entertainers in WWII*. He has since published *Maxims of General Patton*; *I Will be an American Someday Soon* (a citizenship study guide), and biographies on Mark Twain and George Patton.

In 2016, the conflict in Korea threatened to escalate, especially when North Korea boasted of having long-range nuclear missiles that could reach anywhere in the Pacific. As such, interest in the region was a hot topic, so Gary decided it was time to try again with *The Devil's Playground*. He scrapped everything except the journal notes and his photos, and completely rewrote the book, relying on research materials he'd collected since leaving Korea, unclassified documents and interviews by DMZ veterans.

Future projects over the next few years include *The One*, a compilation of first person accounts from military medical personnel, to be published in the Spring of 2020; General George Custer; an update of the WWII entertainers book; a novel on the Iraq War; a novel on the Afghanistan War; *Alive Day*, a compilation of first person accounts from Vietnam vets; and *Women Who Serve*, stories from active duty servicewomen and female veterans.

Gary lives in south Kansas City, with his wife Anita. He helps transitioning service members with their resumes and mentors other veterans writing their own books.